PORTRAITS OF AMERICAN PRESIDENTS, VOLUME II

The Truman Presidency: Intimate Perspectives

Edited by

Kenneth W. Thompson

The White Burkett Miller Center of Public Affairs
University of Virginia

UNIVERSITY
PRESS OF
AMERICA

LANHAM • NEW YORK • LONDON

Copyright © 1984 by

University Press of America,™ Inc.

4720 Boston Way
Lanham, MD 20706

3 Henrietta Street
London WC2E 8LU England

ISBN (Perfect): 0-8191-3699-9
ISBN   (Cloth): 0-8191-3698-0

Co-published by arrangement with
The White Burkett Miller Center of Public Affairs

All University Press of America books are produced on acid-free
paper which exceeds the minimum standards set by the National
Historical Publications and Records Commission.

*Dedicated
to
the Memory
of
President Harry S Truman
and in
commemoration
of the centennial of
his birth
May 8, 1884*

TABLE OF CONTENTS

v

W. AVERELL HARRIMAN

July 20, 1983

Dear Dr. Thompson:

I am pleased to learn that the Miller Center is interested in publishing some of my reflections on activities in the Truman Administration.

In accordance with the agreement reached with the Truman Library, I grant permission to publish my oral history, recorded in 1971, for the Library. It is my understanding that my "essay" will be part of a collection of reminiscences of President Truman and of his Administration.

I am pleased that the White Burkett Miller Center is putting out these "profiles" of our presidents; they are not only interesting but important. My best wishes for continued success,

Sincerely,

Dr. Kenneth W. Thompson
Director
The White Burkett Miller Center
2201 Old Ivy Road
Post Office Box 5707
Charlottesville, VA 22905

cc: Dr. Zobrist
    Truman Library

PREFACE

A pattern has emerged in the course of organizing Miller Center Forums which has led to the present volume. We have discovered that the leading authorities on particular Presidents have helped the Center to draw others with common background to the University of Virginia. By "word of mouth advertising," they have encouraged their friends to come to Faulkner House. Their help has been of inestimable value to a fledgling public affairs center. It has enabled us to further presidential studies through the contributions of distinguished visitors to the understanding of contemporary Presidents.

Partly by accident and partly by design, then, we have discovered our guests were turning the spotlight on certain American Presidents. They were viewing a particular administration from different perspectives and vantage points. The product is a portrait, not a photograph; it helps us see the character and spirit of a leader, not the more or less important details a photograph tends to convey. It tells us what was central to his life and works, not what was peripheral. The photograph reveals what can be seen with the naked eye. The portrait shows one thing the photograph cannot reveal: the human essence of the person portrayed.

With this volume, we continue a series of publications, *Portraits of American Presidents*. We are grateful to the University Press of America for making this series available to a wide audience. We hope the next volume will deal with the presidency of Dwight D. Eisenhower and subsequent volumes with other Presidents. In the Introduction, the editor traces the history of the Center's interest in the presidency of Harry S. Truman.

INTRODUCTION

On May 8, 1984, the country will celebrate the centennial of Harry S. Truman's birth. In preparation for the event, the Miller Center during 1982-83 invited ten of President Truman's most intimate associates and family members to come to Charlottesville to discuss the Truman presidency. Among the participants were: Lucius D. Battle, Clark M. Clifford, Robert J. Donovan, Averell Harriman, Ken Hechler, Frank Pace, John W. Snyder, Elmer B. Staats, John R. Steelman and Francis O. Wilcox. Six were able to accept our invitations while with the others it was necessary to meet them in their offices. Two were kind enough to share papers written for another occasion.

What is common to all those whose impressions make up the present volume is the breadth and scope of their government experience. President Truman, himself a seasoned political leader, apparently preferred aides who had been tested in the crucible of politics. He was not prepared to trust his fate or that of the republic to men who had not had previous political experience.

The theme that runs through all the contributions to this volume is immense respect for the resolve and decisiveness of President Truman. With far less formal education than most of his illustrious colleagues, he demonstrated a grasp of world affairs that few postwar leaders have manifested. By dint of character, he proved he could act when action was required. He showed himself capable of earning and holding the respect of associates and world leaders whose lives had been marked by social and educational advantages denied "the man from Missouri."

The book is divided into four sections. The first section throws the spotlight on Truman's qualities as a leader with contributions by two fellow Missourians who knew him well. Perhaps no living American was closer to President Truman than Clark M. Clifford. He served as speech writer and counsel to the President. He travelled with the President on his whistle stop campaign. No one was more passionately committed to Truman's great foreign policy decisions. John W. Snyder was Secretary of the Treasury and could look back on common military service with the President. His chapter offers a set of personal impressions that help to portray Harry S. Truman's goals and values.

The second section is devoted to a discussion of the Truman White House. John Steelman whom some describe as Truman's chief of staff, although Truman preferred direct contact with his associates, offers firsthand testimony on the organization of the White House and Truman's delegation of power. Ken Hechler who has served in both the executive and legislative branches (he was a nine-term congressman from West Virginia), describes the personnel policies and criteria for selection of staff in the Truman White House.

It is to Truman's foreign policies that many scholars and observers point in seeking to delineate his most enduring accomplishments. The third section in the book focuses on this topic. Respected Truman biographer Robert J. Donovan analyzes his "great foreign policy decisions" and the context in which they were made. Lucius D. Battle, who was Secretary of State Dean Acheson's special assistant, writes on the foreign policy process. Dean Francis O. Wilcox of Johns Hopkins School of Advanced International Studies defends the proposition that bipartisanship in foreign policy was the greatest of all achievements in the Truman presidency.

The final section constitutes, as it were, an appraisal of Truman's political leadership and his concept of the office of the presidency. Frank Pace as Director of the Bureau of the Budget had a unique vantage point for observing the President. Another senior statesman for whom Truman had enormous regard was Governor W. Averell Harriman. Appropriately, the latter concludes our volume with impressions of President Truman's role in the formulation of the Marshall Plan.

Professor Francis Heller, Roy A. Roberts Professor of Law and Political Science at the University of Kansas who assisted President Truman in the writing of his *Memoirs*, has kindly consented to the reprinting of his authoritative and comprehensive essay entitled "Truman" which appeared in the volume *Leaders and Statesmen of the 20th Century*, edited by Lord Longford and Sir John Wheeler-Bennett. The publisher, Sidgwick Jackson of London has given permission for the use of Professor Heller's paper. Heller is a Virginia Ph.D.

I
TRUMAN
AS
LEADER

PRESERVING THE FREE WORLD
Clark Clifford

MR. THOMPSON: Four people who are said to have been closest to and known most about the Truman presidency are: General Marshall, Dean Acheson, you and Averell Harriman. Although we've heard from scholars like Robert Donovan and other observers, we were anxious to get your thoughts about the Truman presidency.

MR. CLIFFORD: Very good. Now I think the best way is for you to ask me questions. I will answer them to the best of my ability. If at any time you wish to explore a subject in greater depth, there must be fourteen or sixteen hours of oral history that I gave to the Truman Library. I must have had four or five visits by the fellow who was head of the Oral History Division of the Truman Library. They probably have interviewed most everybody by this time. But you select any areas that you wish and I'll answer your questions as well as I can remember.

Some young lady called me a while ago because they had received some report that there was a similar type of incident in the Truman administration that you may have read about in the present administration: that a briefing book disappeared from the Carter White House

3

and ended up in the hands of Mr. Reagan's staff, and she said, "Surely, Mr. Clifford, you would remember such an incident," and I said, "I will certainly rack my brain but if you stop and think a moment the year you are talking about is thirty-seven years ago—1946." "Oh," she said, "heavens, I never thought of that." So there will be some gaps in my recollection. Some of the incidents I remember very well because of the drama associated with them. Others were those in which I had been very intimately involved. But proceed with your questions.

MR. THOMPSON: One of the things we've asked everyone who has talked with us is: When did your association begin with President Truman and how did you come into the administration?

MR. CLIFFORD: I came originally from St. Louis. I spent all my life there. It could have been some time in the early forties. I once met Senator Truman. I was one of a large group. He came to St. Louis and there was a reception for him. That's the only other time that I had seen him. He would have had no recollection meeting me because he met three or four hundred people on that occasion. And then later I went into the Navy during the Second World War and I was out some place in the Pacific or maybe Hawaii, and I received word that I was to come to Washington. What had happened was a former client of mine in St. Louis named Vardaman had become naval aide to the President and he learned that he was to accompany President Truman to the Potsdam Conference, and he wanted somebody to look after his office (the naval aide's office) while he was gone. He and the regular Navy did not get on too well. He was a naval reservist and he wanted another naval reservist to come in and look after his office. So I returned and came into San Francisco; I remember it was at the time of the signing of the UN Charter, and he got me a ticket to that. And then I came to the White House (I'm not sure of the date). The President had come in April, somewhere on the 12th or 13th of April, and I came in in June to be assistant naval aide, but mainly to look after the naval aide's office in the White House. And after they returned from Potsdam I would probably go back to my naval post and my headquarters at that time in San Francisco. And that's the way I came in; I really did not know President Truman and he did not know me. But I remember Commander Vardaman, taking me into the Oval Office a morning or two after I had arrived, saying, "Mr. President, this is the young lieutenant who is going to look after my office while we are gone and you will be glad to know he's from St. Louis."

Then they were gone to Potsdam and it was a very long trip. I don't remember what took so long; one reason is that I think they went by ship. Sam Rosenman was counsel at the White House and was grossly overworked. And while they were gone I met Judge Rosenman and said "I'd be so glad to assist you in any way that I could." The functions of the naval aide's office were ceremonial to a great extent, and I knew that my tenure in the navy was limited to the time of the war, and here was Judge Rosenman doing fascinating work over in the other side of the White House. So I said I had time and could I help him. He said I certainly could. So by the time they came back from Potsdam I was giving about one-fifth of my time to the naval aide's office and about four-fifths to Judge Rosenman. So Judge Rosenman said to Vardaman and the President, "Why don't we keep that young fellow here because he's being quite a lot of help to me?" Well, that suited me fine because the White House was a very exciting place to work. So my orders were issued and I stayed there in the naval aide's office.

Gradually my functions began to expand, for I learned and sensed almost from the very beginning that there was a vacuum in the White House. When a President comes in, who has been through an election, he has around him first a small coterie of very close friends of about ten persons, then a little wider circle of about twenty or thirty that he's known for quite a long time, and then outside of that a group of fifty or sixty; it's almost the same for every administration that comes in. And out of that group some of them end up in the White House and some of them end up in Cabinet posts, and some in regulatory agencies. An elected President has a group already formed that he has been working with for four years or eight years or so, and he has a large group from which to pick. When a vice president succeeds to the presidency he doesn't have anybody.

President Truman was having a drink with Sam Rayburn in Sam Rayburn's little separate room on the hill which was called the Board of Education. It was very nice because instead of a senator's secretary saying, "Oh, the Senator is over having a drink with Sam Rayburn," she would say, "Oh, he's over in the Board of Education." So Sam Rayburn occasionally had senators come over and they would drop in at the end of the afternoon, and Senator Truman was there that day. And while he was there and having a drink with Sam the phone rang and he was called to the phone and it was Mrs. Franklin Roosevelt. This is the way the President tells it. I've also heard another report. She said, "Senator Truman?" He said "Yes," and she said, "You must come to the White House at once." He said "At once?" "Yes," she said, "Franklin has died." So of course he immediately goes to the White House. Within an hour the Chief Justice had come, the Cabinet members had assembled and he had become President of the United

States. As vice president, he had three assistants and two or three secretaries, and that was all. So the next morning instead of going to the vice president's office in the Capitol, he goes to the Oval Office. He is President of the United States.

The attitude at the time, on the part of the Roosevelt people was that a lot of them wanted to get out and wanted to get out in a hurry. Franklin Roosevelt was an enormous figure at the time. He had been elected President four times. Vice President Truman had not been brought in to Cabinet meetings, he hadn't been brought in to foreign policy conferences. He served his purpose, in FDR's opinion, by coming from the right part of the country and bringing with him the reputation that he had as an impartial and effective chairman of the War Investigating Committee. The relationship between the two men was not a close one at all. So the Roosevelt people wanted to get out. Here was this man, Roosevelt, with the enormous reputation and in comes a quite unknown senator from Missouri who had certain marks against him. He was a product of the Pendergast machine in Missouri which had gotten quite a bad name. I might say that years later I encountered the same kind of attitude when President Kennedy was assassinated. He had been in office three years, he was very popular and a lot of the Kennedy people wanted out just as quickly as they could get out. In those early days of the Truman administration, every day saw departures. People would go; staff people would leave; Cabinet people would leave. Some of the Cabinet departures didn't upset President Truman at all. He was glad to see some of them go.

But the idea of changing the whole climate from Roosevelt, the intellectual from Groton and Harvard, to a Mid-Westerner whose formal education had ended at high school wasn't what a number of the people wanted. So it was in the very first few days that I learned that the White House was very badly undermanned. Problems would come up and Commander Vardaman would come back and say, "Have you ever written a speech?" I said, "Oh, I guess so." And he said, "Well, we need some speechwriters around here." I said "I sure want to volunteer." Sometime later there was somebody else in the White House who was going to make a speech and didn't know where to turn. So I began to write speeches. After a little while Commander Vardaman came back one day and said, "That last speech you wrote, somebody in the White House liked it and there is going to be a speech meeting this morning. President Truman is going to be with us. Why don't you come along with me?" So it wasn't very long until I became as busy as I could be. Everybody was doing everything that had to be done just to get through each day. After a while there was a vacancy in the Federal Reserve Board and President Truman moved Vardaman, who was a banker, over to the Federal Reserve Board. I had, by that time, developed quite a close relationship with President Truman. It didn't matter who the man was, they just needed manpower around the White House. So I was made naval aide after Vardaman left. There was a lot of joking about it, too, because I had gone from lieutenant junior grade to captain in about a year. You usually remain in grade about six or eight years, so there was a lot of fun being poked at me, which I didn't mind a bit.

So starting out, I remained in the Navy the first half of 1946. But by that time I had become one of the President's speechwriters. Rosenman left the first of January. He had been there many, many years in the Roosevelt administration; he had stayed all through 1945 with the Truman administration and he wanted to get back to the private practice. He was a very loyal and able fellow. So with him gone I was about the only speechwriter in the White House. So I began to write the speeches on a regular basis. That brings you into contact with the President a great deal. We had six months of working together, and in June he called me in and said, "I now want you to get out of the Navy." Both phases of the war were over: the European phase had ended in the spring and then the Japanese phase had ended in August. President Truman said, "I want you to leave the Navy office in the east wing of the White House. I want you to come over and take Rosenman's place. I want you to have Rosenman's office." This was the closest office in the White House next to the President. He said, "I'm doing that because I want everybody to understand that you are succeeding Sam Rosenman." From the time that the President went to Potsdam and I began to work for Sam Rosenman, that's what I hoped would happen. This was one of those rare instances which worked out just right.

I then had four more years with President Truman and I think the relationship developed and grew and deepened during those four years. During that time we went through most everything together.

MR. THOMPSON: You never threatened him. I remember the Bill Moyer's interview in which you spoke about LBJ. Many of the historians revel in calling attention to LBJ's insecurity with regard to high-powered people. President Truman never seemed to have that problem, whether it was Dean Acheson or you or General Marshall, nothing seemed to threaten or make him anxious. Am I right?

MR. CLIFFORD: President Johnson for whom I worked very closely for a number of years had a curious insecurity that President Truman did not have. One could talk a day about that, I guess. Neither one liked the effetism of certain circles in the eastern part of the United States. President Truman didn't cotton up very well to Harvard fellows. It doesn't mean that he didn't want them if he went out to select them, but there had been quite a cult around Roosevelt and he wasn't comfortable with that. He knew that he was always being compared unfavorably to Roosevelt. That, however, did not in any way deter him from selecting the best people that he could get around him, present company excepted. Now, if you stop and think of the men that he brought in: Dean Acheson was an extraordinarily able man—quite sardonic sometimes and peppery, but very able; General Marshall was a very competent man. There were problems with General Marshall over Israel. My own private view was I found him quite inflexible. I found many military men inflexible—quite rigid about positions and rank and protocol. President Truman had a great admiration for Marshall; he would refer to him sometimes as the greatest living American.

President Truman also selected James Forrestal to be the first secretary of defense. I knew Jim Forrestal very well because all the time I was in the naval aide's office he had been secretary of the Navy, and we had a very close liaison and it worked splendidly from the standpoint of the Navy.

The Truman administration was structured to a great extent by the quality of the people whom he brought in to help him in very important positions. He used Averell Harriman a great deal, a wise and experienced man. He went out and searched for the brains, he brought the men in, he worked closely with them and he accepted suggestions from them. I don't mean that he turned the government over to them. He did not. But if he differed with one of these top men, he would say so.

The contrast to that, interestingly enough, was the Jimmy Carter administration. He was an awfully nice fellow, decent, honest, good mind, and he had some of the best press conferences of any President I ever heard. He felt, however, that he and a group of men with the same background as he, coming from one of the rural areas of one of our agricultural states, could come in and operate the White House successfully. It can't be done that way. President Truman had splendid training in government, but he knew from past experience he should get the best men that he could.

When I became counsel in June of 1946, I had established a number of important relationships in the Truman administration, either through the naval aide's office or through other contacts that had been developed, and that proved to be a valuable asset. For instance, I already knew Dean Acheson very well, we had worked together. I already knew Jim Forrestal; we had worked intimately together. And it was in that administration and because of those personal relationships that, to a certain extent, the concept of the national security assistant began to take a vague shape. My major interest was in those fields, foreign policy and national security. And because I knew those two men so well, from time to time, they would talk about their problems, and then after awhile the custom developed that I would go in with them when they came over to see President Truman. That proved to be very valuable. We developed a certain continuity. They would say, "Since the last meeting we had, that matter has taken a little different turn now and I'm sending another memorandum over and if you would just get it to the President."

So that proved to be an exceedingly interesting part of the work and created a different dimension in the office of the counsel. Sam Rosenman had not had those particular contacts that brought me, almost on a daily basis, into those areas. But it worked very well and became a part of the pattern of the operation of the White House. The President did not have any other assistant who fulfilled that capacity. To a certain extent, from a military, standpoint, Admiral Leahy did, but Admiral Leahy and I had become very close friends, when I had been over in the naval aide's office, and we worked together very nicely. Admiral Leahy, to a certain extent, was moving out of the picture as the Second World War concluded. President Truman liked him very much and I think he was quite helpful to the President, but his attitudes were very positive. For instance, I never heard Admiral Leahy refer either to the Russians or to the Soviets; he always referred to them as "those savages." It was useful to know certain key words that were being used in the White House at that time.

That period of time was fascinating. The speechwriting went on, these other duties developed and it proved to be probably as rewarding a period as one could select to be in the White House. It became clear to me at the time, and even more clear as time went on, that President Truman and the United States, in the period from 1945 to 1950, saved the free world.

President Truman's deepest ambition, as the war was ending, was to find a basis of permanent concord with the Soviet Union. We had worked with them so effectively as allies, and he felt that he could work with them to create a lasting peace.

There were only two military strong powers in the world at the end of the Second World War. Europe was prostrate, China amounted to very little. The Soviet Union had a very substantial and powerful military machine, to a great extent because of the aid given by the United States. President Truman, felt after the preliminary meeting that he had had with Stalin in Potsdam, that he could work with him. As you know it started out Stalin and Churchill and Truman but halfway through that conference they had an election in England, and Churchill lost and had to go home and Clement Attlee took his place. The President came back from Europe and, at one of our very first meetings after he got back from Potsdam, he said, "You know, I like old Joe," refering to Stalin. He said, "I think I can get along with him." That was his hope. Well, it was not to be.

As the war was ending, the Soviets embarked upon a period of the most aggressive kind of expansionism, searching for weaknesses, all through the worldwide system of nations. They started in and took control of the countries on their western perimeter—Latvia, Lithuania, Estonia, Bulgaria, Rumania, later Hungary, Czechoslovakia, Yugoslavia. They just took them all by force. The President wanted to work with the Soviets, but they had no interest in that at all. It has been forgotten by most, if they ever knew it, but President Truman offered the Marshall Plan to the Soviet Union so that they might participate. They turned him down.

Then they started the Comintern. They established a communist cell in every country that was of any interest to them and then expanded from that cell. There was hardly a day in the White House but what some new problem didn't come up regarding the Soviet Union. It was a source of the deepest, sincerest regret to him that he couldn't find a basis for getting along with the Soviets, but that was the course they chose. Some revisionists have tried to paint it in a different way, but all I can say is, all they had to do was be there at the time and know what was going on and they would never have gotten such an idea.

So he had to face up to the intransigence of the Soviets, and he did face up to it. Very early in the relationship came a partial confrontation over Trieste and the President took a very firm position on that and the Soviets backed down. And then there was the Berlin airlift. Also we received the message from the British that they could no longer continue the economic and military support of Greece and Turkey. That was a difficult decision he had to make. We had been through the Second World War, we'd lost hundreds of thousands of men, tens of billions of our nation's treasure, and yet here was a situation that he had to face up to. He did. He went up to a joint session of the Congress, I remember it so well because we had worked about three straight nights before he went up there. On March 12, 1947, he delivered a speech in which he enunciated what became known as the

Truman Doctrine. He said, "It shall be the policy of the United States to come to the assistance of those nations who are threatened by communism, either from within or from without." It just sent a surge of hope through the world. It was a speech that echoed around the globe. There wasn't a place in the world that that speech didn't reach because the world at that particular time, in the beginning of 1947, was a perilous place. The Soviets were pushing, pressing all the time. Europe was ready to go down the drain. There wasn't anything left. The British, the French, the Italians, all were bled white.

And then after that came the North Atlantic Treaty Organization in which he said to the Soviets, "If you attack one of the following nations you are attacking the United States. It will be an act of war. Attack them if you will but if you do you are at war with the United States." We had the bomb and nobody else had it. I want to assure you that message rang through the world, too. And interestingly enough, NATO has helped keep the peace for the last thirty-seven years. Then came the greatest of all, the Marshall Plan. An interesting little anecdote: The Marshall Plan was the brainchild of Dean Acheson. I remember talking with him on one occasion. He was imbued with the thought that it had to be done. He talked to President Truman about it and he said, "I have a speaking engagement, and I could try it out." I think it was in Alabama, and the President decided that Dean should go down there and use this concept as a trial balloon. He did and the reaction to it was quite good, rather more favorable than I think either had anticipated. They were worried because it would mean the expenditure of great sums of money and the American people had just been through the agony of the war.

You see, those of us who were in the White House at the time of the close of the war were very sensitive to the feeling in the country. I don't know if you remember, there was hardly anything said about it, but we had a number of riots abroad on the part of American troops who wanted to get home and they felt they weren't getting home soon enough. The concept of the Marshall Plan at the time would cause our people to stick out their chests and square their shoulders and tighten their belts. There were a number of important figures on the hill who said, "Harry, it will never fly."

Dean Acheson went down to Alabama and sent up this trial balloon and it went well. I think that people recognized the seriousness of the times and the opportunity that existed. So we went to work on the speech that would present the plan to the world. I was not quite sure at the time who was going to give it. I remember having a visit with the President and I said, "I think this is going to have a enourmous impact and I hope your name will always be associated with it. I hope it will become known as the Truman concept, for instance." The President replied, "We have a Republican majority in both the Senate and the House and anything that goes up there with Truman's name on it is going to die." He said, "I've been thinking about this, and I agree, this is going to be big and it will have a real impact on the world. I think what we're going to do—I will first talk to Dean about it—is give it to General Marshall and have General Marshall do it. He is completely nonpolitical, he's neither a Democrat or a Republican. He's honored by the American people. Up on the Hill they will attach no political significance to it if General Marshall is associated with it." It was given to General Marshall and he took it over and made a speech at Harvard University. Within two or three days afterwards the newspapers called it the Marshall Plan, and so it was known from then on.

So there is a brief resume of the period as I saw it. I was delighted, years later, in my reading, to come across a statement by Arnold Toynbee, the great British historian, regarded by some as perhaps the world's outstanding historian. He said—this is the general substance of his comment—in later generations the twentieth century will not be remembered as the century in which atomic energy was born, but it will be remembered as that time in which one of the greatest of nations, with no particular hope of any reward or return, saw fit to come to the world's assistance through the Marshall Plan and Point IV. He said, "It seems to me that this is the outstanding event of the century."

Well, I had very much the same feeling. It was so benign in concept and so masterful in its application. The war had caused people in the world to lose hope. The war had gone on so long and the impact on various nations had been so great. The Soviets, for instance, lost twenty million men in the Second World War.

And for the United States to step up and meet these challenges, I think to a great extent, constitutes the reason why, in every year since President Truman went out of office, his reputation in this country and in the world has advanced. It is a reputation for decisiveness, for simplicity, for honesty and for effectiveness. Today we see it as we are engaged in an effort to celebrate the Truman Centennial which will commemorate on May 8, 1984, the hundredth anniversary of his birth. It has become a matter in which the enthusiasm of the people constitute something that's impressive and heartwarming.

I think part of it, too, is that the country has been through a series of traumatic experience. We went through the ghastly tragedy of Vietnam, a war in which many say we never should have been involved. Feeling ran so high, the divisiveness that took place in this country really was tragic. We'd hardly gotten through Vietnam and then we ran into what has become known as Watergate. We went through a crisis in which a President of the United States in effect was on trial.

How many times one has heard over the last eight or ten years, "What we wouldn't give to have Harry Truman back in the White House." You hear it all the time. It's almost a refrain. Also people are picking up little expressions of Harry Truman: "If you can't stand the heat get out of the kitchen"; a sign on his desk which said, "The Buck Stops Here." All that has a great appeal to the American people. And it's greatly in his honor that they feel that way. Every one of those vital decisions now, thirty-five years later, seems to be so logical and so obvious that one thinks that it must not have been very difficult to make. The truth is that every one was very involved and complex. Some tried to stop him at every turn but he decided this was the course of action that he was going to follow.

MR. THOMPSON: Even if we had a Truman today, because SALT is so complicated and because pollution and all the other issues are so much more complex, wouldn't it be hard to sustain bipartisanship and hard to have the clear-cut decisions and simple explanations of the kind he gave? Is there any truth to that view?

MR. CLIFFORD: Not enough truth to warrant giving any time or thought to it. The problems then were so difficult. It was so discouraging, when the war was over, to find the Soviet Union working all the time against what we hoped we might achieve. There was an election in Italy shortly after the war closed that we won by just a hair; the communists might have won it. If President Truman had not saved Greece and Turkey that whole southern anchor in the Mediterranean could have gone down the drain. Without NATO the world would have been very different. It took a lot of courage and a real decisiveness to step into the breach at that time. I've commented on the Marshall Plan. He had a lot working against him. The years 1947 and 1948 were as difficult years as the President ever experienced. He had Republican majorities in the Senate and in the House and they were terribly frustrating years. As he got into 1948, you could search around the country, and particularly in Washington, and it was hard to find anybody who thought Harry Truman had a chance to win in 1948. That campaign was an extraordinarily difficult campaign and he carried the whole load of it. Some of us traveled with him every mile of the way throughout the country. We did it by train, writing speeches—thirteen or fourteen a day—these little back platform comments, and usually a speech in the evening.

As an illustration I remember in the summer of 1948, there were two polling concerns, one was Gallup and one was Roper. Within a few weeks, each of them came out with their last poll showing Dewey maybe as much as 20 or 30 points ahead of Harry Truman, and each of them said there was no use in having any more polls. Dewey was so far ahead and gaining all the time that the election was a foregone conclusion. It was very tough to take. Everything on the Dewey train was going just the way it should; everything on the Truman train was one difficulty after another. We got down to Oklahoma City. He was going to make a nationwide radio address that night on foreign policy, and the network said, "Mr. President, you cannot go on the air unless you pay in advance." Calls had to be made to some wealthy people in New York and they came through and the amount was gathered during the day with the President not knowing whether he was going to go on the air or not that night. It was really rough, it was tough.

A month before the election *Newsweek* came out with its lead article, saying they had selected the fifty top political experts in the country and had sent them a simple ballot which said, "In your opinion which man will win, Dewey or Truman?" It received a lot of attention because these men were all the top men—Walter Lippmann, Roscoe Drummond, the Alsop brothers and the like. It was an interesting story, it was an intriguing thing for them to do. So we waited with bated breath.

A week before the election, *Newsweek* was to announce the results of the poll. We were some place in North Dakota, and as our train came in I remember swinging off the step and going in to the station to find out if they had a newsstand and they did. There on the cover of *Newsweek* were the results of the poll and it had Truman and the number of votes that he received, and Dewey and the number of votes that he got. Truman zero, Dewey fifty. All fifty had replied and all fifty said Dewey was going to win. I got back on the private car and walked through the livingroom part of the car and I put the magazine under my coat. As I walked through the President was sitting there reading and he looked up and said, "What does it say?" So I walked on and said, "Good morning, Mr. President." He repeated, "What does it say?" I certainly did not want to be the one to show it to him, and I said, "What does what say?" He said, "I saw you get off the train and I saw you go in and there's a newsstand, and I'm assuming that you've got an issue of *Newsweek* with you." I had no alternative but to bring the magazine out and hand it to him. He said not a word, but showed no indication of discouragement. He had an inner conviction he would win.

He had a lot of decisions to make in that campaign, a lot of mean decisions. I'm answering your question: Were things simpler then? They weren't simpler then at all. In each period of history, it seems to me, the people at that time think their problems are the most complex that ever existed. The President stayed right on course through that trying time. He fought even harder during the last ten days of that campaign. Something was happening, we did not know what. The crowds were bigger, they gathered down in the railroad yards earlier, there would be two or three thousand of them who would turn out in the yards. He'd start and he'd get going and, about two or three minutes into a speech, someone would yell, "Give 'em hell, Harry," and then the whole crowd would pick it up. If after a while it didn't come from the crowd, sometimes I think it's possible that somebody on the train might have slipped out and yelled "Give 'em hell, Harry." But it tickled the crowd a lot, and he would give them his best.

There were three great issues that he had. Over and over he would emphasize those three leading issues. One was labor. The Republicans had gotten in control of Congress and in their two years in office they had passed the Taft-Hartley Bill. We called it the Slave Labor Act. We used it many time with working people all over the country and used it very effectively. The next one was with the blacks. He'd really gone to bat for the blacks. He had a civil rights program and fought for it. He lost five southern states to Strom Thurmond. The conservatives organized a new party and he lost those states. But he fought hard, and it was a good issue.

And then as far as the farmers were concerned we got the break of all time. It was a minor issue at first. The Republican majority in Congress wanted to do something for their supporters after having been out for sixteen years. The grain warehouse interests had gone up to the Congress and had gotten them to pass a bill which provided that a farmer could get the support prices for his grain only if the grain were deposited in a licensed warehouse. That was great for the warehouse industry, I dare say. It turned out to be a bum deal for the farmers because the Lord smiled on the Democrats that year. The sun and the rain came at the right time and we had an enormous corn crop and an enormous wheat crop. And in no time at all, you see, the grain elevators in the country were filled to bursting and the farmer had to pile his grain on his own premises and he could get (I'm picking the figures at random) $4.50 if he put it in an elevator, and about $2.80 or $3.00 if he couldn't get the support price for his grain.

We went out to the plowing contest in Dexter, Iowa. I think we launched it then and the President said to the farmers: "This is the kind of treatment you get from this Republican Congress. They are always interested in the vested interests. GOP stands for Gluttons Of Privilege." And it rang out around the country, GOP, Gluttons Of Privilege. He said, "The Republican party has plunged a pitchfork into the farmer's back." Pretty lurid language, but I want to tell you it was telling stuff. We went back and forth through the great Middle West telling this story and every farmer could understand it and every shopkeeper could understand it because they all knew what had happened. The fact is that if you could get support price for some grain and not for the others, the Republicans had done it. Dewey and his crowd didn't pay much atttention to it. They didn't think it amounted to very much. We thought it did. So on that last ten days of the campaign the excitement was picking up. The enthusiasm was growing and it carried him right on. I never heard President Truman at any time offer the slightest suggestion that he wasn't going to win. What he felt in the deep recesses of his heart I do not know, for he never let on to anybody else. The night of the election it got to be two or three o'clock in the morning, and the whole election came down to Michigan, Ohio, California, and Illinois, and returns would dribble in, a little more and a little more, and finally they all came in. Illinois went for Truman and Michigan went for Truman and Ohio went for Truman and then along about four o'clock in the morning California went for Truman. He carried them all. So as a matter of fact, when you finally looked at the electoral vote, he had won by a comfortable margin. He'd carried all of those big states.

When one evaluates the Truman administration, you find an administration that carried out one of the most successful programs in foreign policy of any administration. As far as his domestic policy was concerned, President Truman fought for a strongly liberal program; he was interested in the little fellow and in the underdog. He did everything in his power to help the underprivileged. I really didn't know until years and years later the enormous impact of an executive order that he had issued in which he eliminated all kinds of discrimination that existed in the military services as far as blacks were concerned. I went over to the Pentagon later on in the Johnson adminstration and I found that discrimination because of color no longer existed. It was a very, very strong executive order.

So here's a man who succeeded in foreign policy and domestic policy; who conducted that marvelous fight in 1948 that began to appeal to the

American people and they said, "This man's for us," and to this very day that has been the feeling of the American people.

MR. THOMPSON: May I ask just one final footnote question? It's not to take away from anything you've said. It really is asking whether there is an explanation of another strength that he had. It concerns the story of Paul Hoffman's appointment as ECA administrator. When President Truman asked Hoffman to accept the new post, he said, "I have to go home and talk to my wife." If the story is not apocryphal, President Truman immediately called a press conference and said Hoffman had been appointed ECA administrator. He said he did it to save Mrs. Hoffman the pain of having to worry with her husband about the appointment all week long. There is just a little glimmer of a political skill comparable to the kind of thing that the revisionists are now saying President Eisenhower had, the hidden hand theory, with a President we thought wasn't political at all. Truman used to go around to liberal arts colleges and other places and lecture about politics, and he said, "The best politics is to do what's right." What you've said is a demonstration of that. This Hoffman story and a few small things suggest that he was not oblivious to strategic and political moves.

MR. CLIFFORD: I had not intended, by devoting myself to the great issues of his day, to suggest that he wasn't a political animal. He had grown up in politics—it was his whole background. He had grown up in Missouri politics, had become what was called a county judge, which in Missouri was a county administrator. That was just the term that was used. So he understood politics. He believed in it and he believed that the Democratic party was vastly superior to the Republican party and that the country had made its real progress under the Democratic party. He said, "Every now and then I would ask of some person, 'Are you a Republican or a Democrat? If the person says, 'I'm an Independent,' then I know he's against me."

In the great decisions that he made, he sensed and he had it within himself to see that there was no real politics in those. He felt they had to be done. He was politically astute enough, as I previously mentioned, to be sure that the Marshall Plan was not attributed to him because he knew that would sound the death knell of the plan. We went through a very difficult time involving Israel in 1947 and 1948, and it has been suggested by certain revisionists that some of the decisions that he made with reference to Israel were political decisions. I've been asked that a number of times and I've said that every single decision that a President makes, if it's a decision of any significance, has *some* political impact—every single one. Watch the decisions being made to-day by President Reagan, whether it's on education or disarmament, whether it's on the environmental issue or Central America, everything has some political cast to it. But that doesn't mean that a President makes decisions based wholly on politics.

President Truman fought for Israel and he fought hard. He had to fight against his own State Department. Day in and day out on this issue, they were undercutting him all the time. He had to fight against the Defense Department. Jim Forrestal talking to me one time said, "Clark, you don't understand Israel. The situation involving Israel is a mathematical problem." I said, "Mathematical problem? What do you mean?" He said, "There are 350,000 Jews and there are 35 million Arabs, and the 35 million Arabs are going to push the 350,000 Jews into the Mediterranean and that's going to be the end of it."

The ethical and moral, humanitarian and sentimental reactions that the President felt toward Israel were very, very important to him. We talked a lot about it, we felt the same way about it. I know why he fought for Israel. I know that, for instance, he believed that in the Old Testament there were references to the fact that ultimately there would be a Jewish homeland. He felt that the Jews were entitled to a their own homeland. After the Second World War there were millions of displaced people and they all had some place to go to except the Jews and he was very conscious of it. Then he felt a certain sense of guilt, as all right-thinking human beings did after the war, to learn that six million Jews had been murdered in the Third Reich. Why couldn't this have been stopped in some way? Also he felt very strongly that the British had promised the Jews a homeland in what had become known many years before, back in 1917, as the Balfour Declaration. He felt very strongly in that regard. He felt a desire to see that these people who had been so mistreated all through their lives and all through their history would be given a chance. That's why he fought continually for what was known as "partition" in the UN and fought against "trusteeship," which is what the British wanted because they wished to avoid the decision. Finally, the showdown came. He wished to recognize the new state of Israel. He wanted the United States to be the first nation to recognize Israel. General Marshall was adamantly op-posed to it. That's another long story but we went through some very bitter, trying times at that stage but he just stuck with his position. Eleven minutes after the Jewish homeland announced that it was a new nation and named itself Israel the United States recognized Israel. By that time he had brought General Marshall along and General Marshall at least did not oppose it.

Harry Truman believed in his God, in his country and in himself. His life turned out to be a signal success because of his honesty, his courage and the illustrious service he rendered to this nation and to the world. I have often thought that his life and career were personified in a remark his mother made many years ago. She said, "Harry could plow the straightest furrow in Jackson County." I believe that says it all.

MR. THOMPSON: That was just wonderful.

VIEWS OF A FELLOW
MISSOURIAN*
John W. Snyder

At nine o'clock on the morning of April 14, 1945, I walked into the office of the new President of the United States. And within an hour my whole life's plan for the future was completely changed. . . .

At noon on April 12, 1945, I was in Mexico City. A joint group of United States—Mexican bankers had just concluded a successful conference on exchange rates concerning our export-import business.

Floyd Ransom, a prominent American businessman in Mexico City, had invited a number of the conference participants to his home for a luncheon to celebrate our significant accomplishment. It turned out to be a typical Mexican luncheon that lasted the remainder of the afternoon.

We were still at the table when the butler announced that the radio had just flashed the story of President Roosevelt's death.

A. P. Giannini, the founder of the Bank of America, was sitting next to me, and had been inquiring about the background of the Vice President, as there had been numerous rumors on the West Coast regarding Roosevelt's health.

*John W. Snyder was Secretary of the Treasury, Federal Loan Administrator and Director of the Office of War Mobilization and Reconversion in the Truman administration. He presented these reflections on the 25th Anniversary of Truman's succession to the presidency. He has kindly given permission for their use in this volume.

The announcement had the effect of a startling explosion, which started everyone to talking at once. There was great speculation as to what sort of President Mr. Truman would make and because of my long friendship with him I was piled with many questions.

Due to my close observation of his activities as a military leader, county court official, senator, and chairman of the Truman Committee, I talked particularly about his great skill in choosing men of experience in connection with the individual task that he was working on at any given time. This facet of Mr. Truman's makeup greatly impressed Giannini. He made one remark, "I really feel better."

Later in the evening at the Reforma Hotel, I talked with President Truman by phone, telling him how greatly shocked we all were to learn of Roosevelt's death. "Yes," he said, "I feel like I have been struck by a bolt of lightning." I went on to assure him of my deepest sympathy in the trying hours he was experiencing. He broke in to ask how soon I could get to Washington. I said that I would be there at the earliest possible moment. The conversation ended with his telling me, "Come to see me as soon as you get here."

I finally arrived in Washington at 10:40 p.m., the night of April 13th. It had been a sad, depressing trip across the country. At each stop we made, the terminal was filled with dazed apprehensive mourners lamenting the death of a great leader.

The next morning, April 14, I was on the way for my first visit with *President* Truman. I can assure you that it was in a prayerful mood that I approached my appointment with a man who so richly deserved the fullest and the most earnest support of every citizen of our country, and for that matter, of the world.

In spite of the problems that had been piling in on him, I was pleased to see that the President appeared to have had a good night's rest and was confidently taking up his myriad tasks.

He spent about fifteen minutes bringing me up to date. The first official act had been to declare a national mourning period and in making arrangements for the White House funeral rites of President Roosevelt. He had talked with his Cabinet, with leaders of Congress, advised foreign heads of state, conferred with the Secretary of State to receive information reports on foreign matters, including the war posture. He had met with Admiral Leahy and the military leaders, including the Secretaries of War and Navy, he had arranged to address a joint session of Congress on April 16. Throughout the day he had received messages from all over the world and had had a visit with Jimmy Byrnes. He was learning that he had not been kept informed on critical matters by his predecessor. He also had learned the day before for the first time that Stalin was not living up to the agreements that he had made with Churchill and Roosevelt. A matter that greatly distressed President Truman was the unhappy complications which were developing in the Polish situation. He said that he had spent some hours the evening before reading the position papers on this development.

That morning before I arrived he had already talked to Steve Early and Sam Rosenman about his forthcoming speech before Congress. Another matter that he must decide that day was about the final arrangements for the United Nations Conference which had been scheduled in San Francisco for that month.

Frankly, I was appalled at the volume of matters that he had acted on in the few hours since he had been sworn in.

He then told me that he wanted me to be in Washington with him. The day before he had checked for a suitable assignment and had learned that the job of Federal Loan Administrator was vacant. So he wanted me to take that one immediately. Personally, I felt that I could be of far great help as the president of the First National Bank in St. Louis, a position that I had been elected to assume on July 1. We were still discussing the matter when Jim Byrnes came in. He told Jim that I was holding out on the appointment. Jimmy spoke up and said, "Harry, don't forget who you are now. Order him to do it." That ended the discussion. Three days later, on April 17, the President sent my nomination as Federal Loan Administrator to the Senate as his first major appointment.

As I was leaving, Secretary Morgenthau came in for a very short call.

Another day's heavy schedule was ahead for the new President.

At four p.m. James Byrnes and I proceeded to the East Room of the White House to attend the simple funeral rites of a great President. The service was conducted by Bishop Angus Dunn. A few words by the bishop, some of President Roosevelt's favorite hymns were sung, and the service was over. The brevity was at the request of Mrs. Roosevelt.

President Truman, Mrs. Truman and Margaret went to Hyde Park for the services there. I met the train upon its return Sunday evening and rode with the Trumans to their Connecticut Avenue apartment. En route we discussed the speech which he was to deliver before the joint session of Congress the next day. I was pleased with what he planned to say. We changed one or two parts and decided to add a couple of thoughts to emphasize that the war was not yet over and to touch on the U. S. role after the war.

I left him at the apartment with the understanding that I would be at the White House early the next morning.

On Monday morning I had an opportunity to go over the full draft of the speech and later went with the President to the Capitol to hear him deliver it. It was well received—at one point with a standing ovation, when he reasserted the demand for an unconditional surrender.

I saw President Truman two or three times a day during the week. I had lunch with him, Vaughan and Ed McKim at the Blair House. This was quite a reunion from old Fort Riley days during the twenties and thirties when as colonels, Truman commanded the 379th F. A. Reserve Regiment, Vaughan the 380th and I the 381st, for two weeks each summer. I recall this military phase as it was in those days that Colonel Truman and I began to apply the Five Paragraph Military Order to problems in our civilian life. To refresh your memory, the Five Paragraph Order requires:

1. Situation
   a. Enemy Forces (Elements working against us)
   b. Own Forces (Resources we have available)

2. Mission
   (What we are trying to do)

3. Solution
   (How can we handle problems)

4. Administration and Logistics
   (Implementation of our resources)

5. Order and Communication
   (Retained direction)
   (Delegated direction)
   (Line of authority)

I know that formula was of great value to our President in the critical first months, as it was throughout his entire administration.

A delightful incident occurred as we were returning to the White House. As we reached the center of Pennsylvania Avenue, the President suddenly stopped and said, "Oh, hell! I left my White House pass on the dresser."

Tuesday morning, the 16th, among other matters we discussed the world's critical food situation. I took the occasion to mention former President Hoover's experience after W.W. I. I had met him in Paris in 1919. Others thought well of the idea, and some time later Mr. Truman called him to the White House to discuss Europe. This led to his appointment by the President, as honorary chairman, Famine Emergency Committee. They became warm friends. Years later when I was talking with President Hoover, he said that the appointment added ten years to his life.

The President spent some minutes in discussing the problems that would follow the fall of Hitler. He felt, from reports, that victory was imminent in Europe. There were many matters that would require conferences with Churchill and with Stalin. He was most interested in meeting Churchill, though he did not wish to offend Stalin by a premature talk with the British. It was a delicate situation about which he was seeking diplomatic advice. He was considerably concerned about the organization of the occupation of Germany, the logistics of some withdrawal of troops, and the reenforcement of the forces in the Pacific. He told me that he had learned something that might materially affect the Pacific situation but was not in position to discuss it yet. (It was his first knowledge of the *atom bomb*.)

Later that morning, I attended the President's first press and radio conference at 10:30 a.m. President Truman had, with the assistance of Steve Early and others, prepared a set of rules of conduct for future press conferences. As they were somewhat similar to those of his predecessor they were accepted without discussion and after a few announcements covering White House staff, a letter from Mrs. Roosevelt, and one or two other matters, he said he was ready for questions. Everything went well, although the President passed up a few questions that he preferred to discuss at a more appropriate time.

The Trumans moved to the Blair House that day.

The night of the 17th, the President made a worldwide broadcast to the U. S. Armed Forces in foreign service.

The warmth, understanding and courage conveyed by this message was reassuring to the troops around the world that they were under the continued leadership of a dedicated commander.

The remainder of the week I spent considerable time on the Hill and at the RFC. The hearing on Friday was relatively short as most of the committee had had me before them numerous times during defense plant days and already knew my policies.

I had off-the-record visits with President Truman on Saturday and Sunday. In summing up the week, he felt that making the final arrangements for the United Nations Conference in San Francisco, the study and discussions of the food problem, his budget discussions with Harold Smith, the talks on the polish problem, his talks with Secretary of State Stettinius, Ambassador Harriman and State Department experts on the perfidy of Stalin, his first friendly cooperative talk with Molotov: all of these discussions were most helpful to him in making the decisions he had had to make quickly. He confided that although he had communicated with Churchill several times during the week, he was most anxious to meet him. He added that he was greatly pleased with his first speech to Congress, its reception and his first press conference.

The President told me that he was particularly pleased with his talk with Harriman who had flown back from Moscow for the conference. "Harriman knows what he is talking about," he remarked. "He is well informed on the Polish situation. His views on Stalin were most revealing. His dispatches, which I have carfully read are frank and to the point." He grinned when he told me that Harriman had been fearful that he had not read his reports and would not, therefore, fully understand the situations. "I told him," he said, "that if he sent in good reports, I would always read them carefully."

Incidentally, the attitude of Molotov completely toughened in the later talk Monday when President Truman forcefully insisted that the Polish agreements arrived at in Yalta should be carried out. I was told by Ambassador Harriman later that the President was very firm in his talk with Molotov, insisting that Russia live up to her agreements.

I would like to inject here that it was Ambassador Harriman who advised Jesse Jones and me on one of his visits to Washington in 1943 that Stalin was not trustworthy about all of his agreements.

During one of our talks, the President said that he thought that he would take his time about making major changes in personnel. He strongly felt that as President Roosevelt had been elected to the presidency by a substantial majority only five months before, he, Truman, should carry out, to the best of his ability, the policies on which Roosevelt had been elected. He believed that Cabinet members and staff who were close to the former President could help him materially in learning about those commitments. He had asked all Cabinet members to stay on. He said, however, that he had already asked Jim Byrnes, off the record, to be Secretary of State, after the United Nations meeting. He worried about presidential succession. He considered that Byrnes would be highly qualified.

He told me then that he knew that Frank Walker, the Postmaster General, wanted to quit due to health reasons. He had been trying to leave for some time. He further felt that Francis Biddle, Miss Perkins and Claude Wickard would also like to be relieved. He hoped none would want to leave until the war situation was clearer. "I want to talk to Sam Rosenman, Fred Vinson and you about those three, as I have someone in mind for each of those posts. I'm not too sure of Ickes." I spoke up to say that Ickes had been very cooperative with DPC in furnishing power for the light metals reduction plants. "Yes," he said, "he is a good man, but I am afraid that he will not always remember who is boss. Anyway, I am not ready to make a change there yet," he added. He then said that he also wanted to talk with me about the Treasury, as he was not pleased with some of Morganthau's positions. I promptly brought up Fred Vinson's name, as I immediately thought of the tax problems that would confront the administration. When asked how will I knew him, I had to confess that my acquaintance was largely by reputation, but that he appeared to have considerable political charisma. Frankly, I didn't use that word as it hadn't been liberated at the time.

Mr. Truman said he had thought of him—and one or two others. We were interrupted about that time and further discussions had to be postponed.

I left early the next day, Monday, for St. Louis to terminate my First National Bank connection, and make peace with my family.

In light of what has happened to some presidential nominations recently, I probably was a little over-confident. The Senate, however, saved me by unanimously approving my appointment the next day, Tuesday, April 24th.

I remained in St. Louis four days in closing matters at the bank and in arranging to bring my family to Washington. Walter Smith, then president of the St. Louis bank, said he would not hurry in replacing me in the hope that I might be able to get back soon. With that same hope in mind, we stored our furniture and planned to bring only a few things to Washington. It turned out that the few months stretched out into eight years, and I never got back to St. Louis.

I arrived back in Washington at 10:30 a.m. on April 30th and was sworn in at the White House at two-thirty that afternoon. And there I was, back in government service again. My face was really quite reddened when I received a telegram from Giannini saying, "I see that Truman is following his old policy in selecting men."

President Truman was present at the swearing-in. He called me into his office and told me not to get so tied up at the RFC that I wouldn't show up regularly for informal talks. "I want you around where I can talk with you or I wouldn't have brought you back here."

It was at that time that we made an agreement that we kept through three jobs and nearly eight years of time. We would keep my name off of the calendar when I came to see him. As a result our visits were mostly off-the-record except on rare occasions. . . .

On July 1, 1945, the first Cabinet changes were made: Tom Clark, Clint Anderson, Bob Hannegan and Lou Schwellenbach were sworn in. On July 3, 1945, James Byrnes became Secretary of State. On July 23, 1945, Fred Vinson became Secretary of the Treasury, and I became Director of Office of War Moblization and Reconversion.

In those early days, when pressures were greatest, President Truman came in contact intimately with a number of able, effective leaders with whom he had had only casual acquaintances before. The foundations were laid then for friendships that have lasted through good days and bad for twenty-five years—among those I would like to name two . . . whose help, advice and encouragement were a great comfort to President Truman. They are Ambassador Harriman and Secretary Acheson.

Let us pause for a moment to catalog some of the blockbusting experiences and the attendant decisions that had to be made by President Truman in the first four months of his presidency, ending with the surrender of Japan.

In his splendid book on the Truman administration, *Present At the Creation*, Dean Acheson ventured that Mr. Truman learned fast. This is really quite an understatement when you consider that on April 12, 1945, Harry S. Truman was suddenly catapulted from the relatively peaceful atmosphere of the Senate into the seething caldron of exploding events in the midst of a war about which he had not been briefed.

To this day I am still filled with pride and admiration at the amazing speed with which President Truman assimilated the huge piles of information about hitherto unknown, to him, facts, situations, figures and personalities, and came through promptly with scores of sound decisions.

Consider for a moment of suddenly being made aware:

1. That you were the President of the United States,

2. Of the necessity to assure continuity of the function of the entire U. S. responsibilities—orient with Cabinet—with staff—with Congress—with foreign powers,

3. Communicate with troops in the field all over the world,

4. Take up share of direction of a world war,

5. Assimilate the vast amount of information covering diplomatic arrangements, including briefings on heads of state, foreign ambassadors here and ours abroad,

6. Consider changes in Cabinet,

7. Carry on discussions and plans for the war with people you had never met or communicated with before,

8. Arrange to quietly learn if any unrecorded commitments had been made to the British or to the Russians,

9. Address the close of United Nations Conference, June 26th, 1945.

10. In three weeks face the countless problems of the surrender of the Germans, May 8th, 1946,

11. Arrange and attend the Potsdam Conference,

12. The change of British prime ministers in the midst of the Potsdam Conference,

13. The decision to drop the atom bomb,

14. And square off for the decisions brought on by V-J Day.

Yes, those four months were busy days for the President.

It was fortunate, as I have said, that he was able to quickly recruit able talent to help him bear the burden of those and later days.

I am impelled to tell you of a few of those whose names stand out, to me, in their invaluable aid to President Truman during those early months.

I have listed them alphabetically, as it is impossible to apply priorities to wholehearted superb all-essential thoughts and deeds.

Dean Acheson—Early assistance in State briefing and position papers. He earned his salt in later days.

Alben Barkley on congressional matters.

James Byrnes on Roosevelt, Teheran, Yalta-Potsdam.

William Clayton on European food situation and pending economic crisis.

Winston Churchill—Early communications, Stalin, Potsdam negotiations.

Joseph Davies—for his trip to see Churchill.

Steve Early—White House, Roosevelt, press.

General Dwight Eisenhower—Military and civilian matters in Europe.

James Forrestal—Military and naval briefings.

W. Averell Harriman—Stalin, Russia, Poland, diplomatic matters.

Harry Hopkins—Roosevelt, trip for Truman to see Stalin.

Admiral William D. Leahy—War posture, military counsel, knowledgeable appraisals.

General George Marshall—Military genius, great statesman, diplomat.

Sam Rayburn—Congressional matters, advice.

Sam Rosenman—Roosevelt, legal, speeches, advice.

Charles Ross—Press, counsel, dependable information.

Edward Stettinius—State Department briefings.

Henry Stimson—War situation, atom bomb.

Fred Vinson—Politics, taxes, domestic economy, consultant.

And, of course, his top source of strength—Bess Truman.

There were doubtless others, but these are the ones I find mentioned prominently in my notes of those days who seemed to be effectively helping shoulder the load. One or two that I have mentioned disappointed the President later, but that doesn't detract from their early assistance.

In closing I want to give you a few of my impressions of the strengths of Mr. Truman that stood him in good stead in meeting the tremendous demands on his courage, strength, faith and character in that testing period of heart and mind.

There were many facets to Mr. Truman's make-up that enabled him to make decisions promptly:

1. His capacity to quickly classify, weigh and make use of facts presented to him.

2. His choice of counsellors on specific matters.

3. His instinctive ability to sort out essentials.

The President was once asked if he had ever regretted having made a major decision. His reply was revealing, "Events followed events so closely that there were many things that had to be done almost instantly as a delay might have been disastrous. Had I had more time to contemplate some of the matters they might have been handled in some other way. But considering the information available at the time and the circumstances prevailing when the decisions had to be made, I do not see how I could have acted very differently."

President Truman once taught me a most valuable lesson the principle of which, without doubt, enabled him to carry his great burdens with such composure.

He told me that when he was preparing for bed at night he would searchingly ask himself whether or not he had acted on matters of the day to the best of his abilities. If the answer was in the affirmative he went soundly to sleep and awakened the next morning refreshed, and ready for the day's trials.

Dean Acheson in speaking of Truman some years after the close of the Truman administration said, "If a President will make a decision, you're in luck. That is the essential quality. And if he has a high batting average in the correctness of his decisions, then you're in clover."

As to the quality of President Truman's decisions there was never any doubt.

Eric Sevareid summed up my remarks for me when he wrote:

"Chance, in good part, took Harry Truman to the presidency, but it was his character, his simplicity, his honesty and his self-discipline that kept him there and determined his historical fate. He is, without any doubt, destined to live in the books as one of the strongest and most decisive of the American Presidents."

II
THE
TRUMAN
WHITE
HOUSE

THE PRESIDENTIAL ASSISTANT
John Steelman

MR. THOMPSON: It's a great pleasure to welcome you to the third of the Truman discussions we've had this week. John Steelman served as director of the United States Conciliation Service under President Franklin D. Roosevelt. He became special assistant to President Truman on President Truman's accession to office. He was the last director of the Office of War Mobilization and Reconversion, whose work I believe came to an end in 1946. If he had held the position he held in the Truman administration today he would have been called chief of staff. At that time the position was referred to as the assistant to the President of the United States. In all of these positions he had a unique opportunity to observe President Truman, to talk with him, and share ideas and concerns, and to come to some conclusions about President Truman as a leader and also as a person. And it is in that connection that we're particularly pleased that he is a part of the small group who have been helping us with a Truman Portrait in these months preceding the Truman centennial. As you know the centennial is to be in May of 1984 commemorating Truman's birth. It helps us to look back on that important presidency and enables everyone to see what were his great accomplishments, and what were his problems and what were his limitations. It is a great honor to have John Steelman with us this afternoon.

MR. STEELMAN: Thank you, Mr. Thompson. He's really gotten you folks in for trouble. It will take me at least five hours to tell you about my associations with President Truman. On second thought maybe I ought to give you a few highlights and let you ask me questions. First he suggested I tell you a little about how I came to be associated with President Truman. As Mr. Thompson mentioned, I was director of U.S. Conciliation Service under Mr. Roosevelt and my job was to settle strikes. President Truman later gave me credit for winning the war which was a slight exaggeration. He said, "If you hadn't kept the folks at work we would have lost the war." I think we handled some 81,000 labor disputes during my term involving over 40 million workers. The worst time we had was during that little period when Hitler and Russia were allies. We had some real tough ones in this country during those days. Later, after Hitler double-crossed his ally, Russia, and Russia got over on our side it was easier.

How I came to be associated then with President Truman, I had left President Roosevelt in 1944, the first day after the election. He wouldn't let me go till then. I decided it was time to go the New York and make a little money, so I was gone. President Roosevelt knew he would not live out his term. He knew he was selecting the next President of the United States when he asked—not only asked—forced Senator Truman to be his running mate. So, sure enough he passed away and Vice President Truman became President. He first sent an emissary to New York to feel me out on being secretary of commerce or secretary of labor, and I declined. About a week or two later I got a telephone call, "The President wants to see you personally." So I said, "Well, I'll be down in a couple of days."

I went in to see President Truman and he said, "I'm going to do to you what President Roosevelt did to me." He said, "President Roosevelt said, 'Are you going to do what I'm asking you to do or are you going to let your country down?'" The senator had to say, "Yes." The President said, "I'm saying the same to you." He said, "You've been around here for twelve years, you know everybody—all the senators and congressmen, and the newspaper people know you and like you, you've done all of them favors, you never made any of them mad."

Then he said, "Look at me, here I am in a position I didn't want, I didn't ask for, but here I am in a position that's too big for me." He said, "In fact I think it's too big for anybody but I know it's too big for me. I need help, help, help, and you've got to help me." So I made a deal to work for him for six months which ended up six months after Eisenhower's election. My six months never got over. About once a year I'd say, "Mr. President, I was glancing at the calendar last night and it seemed to me that, unless I looked at the wrong page, my six months are almost up. My office in New York is suffering." "Oh no," he would say, "the six months aren't up yet, we've got to do so and so first." So that went on and on. Anyhow, that's how I came to be associated with him. I didn't know he knew me. I said, "I didn't know you knew me, Mr. President," and he said, "Oh, I had my eye on you all during the war. If it hadn't been for you we'd have lost it. You kept the boys at work." So he said, "I need help. You've got to help me."

Sometime later, after I had served as special assistant for a while, I was appointed director of the Office of War Mobilization and Reconversion. I got the reconversion end of it because the war had just ended. That was the most powerful job Congress ever created. I had legal authority to issue orders to the President's Cabinet. Well, you mentioned that the office ended in 1946. The way it ended is interesting. President Truman had learned that he could sign anything I handed him. It had been double-checked forty times and there was no use to read it. So I took a great stack of papers for the President to sign and he'd sign them and hand them back and on the bottom one was abolishing my job. He signed that and I said, "Mr. President, maybe you ought to glance at this last one because there may be some questions raised about it." Reading what he had signed he said, "Does this mean what I think it does?" and I said, "Yes." He said, "You don't think the job of coordinating the executive branch of the government has ended, do you?" and I said, "Mr. President, we should live so long. It never will be completed, but nobody should be between you and your Cabinet, certainly in peacetime. I've issued about six orders to members of your Cabinet since I've had the job for six months, but in every instance I got an agreement first. We all understood it." So I said, "I don't need this kind of authority." "Well," he said, "I tell you what; I'll leave this signed if you'll stay with me and keep doing exactly what you're doing now." So that's where the title the assistant to the President arose. From then on I was speaking for him, not myself. But the job was exactly the same.

Well, anyway, we were sitting on the beach down in Key West one day, discussing some official who had gotten out of line, he was taking himself too seriously. He thought the world couldn't operate without him. At this point President Truman gave me the idea that Presidents are human after all. He said, "Here we sit, just think what a great country we have. A farmer boy from Missouri, another farmer boy from

Arkansas, and here we are, the two most powerful jobs in the world.''
But he said, ''Do you realize if we went swimming right out there and
we both drowned, this great country would go right along without
us?'' So he said, ''Who does he think he is? If you can't straighten him
out when we get back to Washington we'll have to let him go.'' So I
got this idea that Presidents are just human after all.

You know I got interested in the subject, I went way back even to
George Washington. You know George was our first President and we
revered him; we idolized him because the people who came here from
Europe were accustomed to kings and emperors. So here's President
George Washington. But George was just human after all. George
once said, ''I've been called a delinquent.'' He didn't say who, but it
was his mother presumably. His mother said, ''George is off playing
general when he ought to be here at home taking care of his mother.''
So he was human after all, but we idolized him. I studied the
Presidents all the way down, but here I will mention only a few.

President Harding was human. He was influenced by his wife. Congress passed a law to build a home for the vice president. Vice Presi-
dent Coolidge and Grace lived across the street in the old Willard
Hotel. Florence Harding didn't like the Coolidges. She referred to
them as ''those Coolidges.'' Florence persuaded the President to veto
the bill. A few weeks later President Harding went on a trip to the
West Coast and died. Grace waited a week or ten days and called
Florence up and said, ''When can you move out of the White House?
We're moving in.'' So instead of a new house they got the White
House itself.

President Hoover was thought to be a very strict, correct person,
but he was human, too. He lived the longest of any ex-President, by
the way, ninety years. He was an old friend of mine from college days.
Roosevelt never invited him back to the White House. I got him and
President Truman together and he used to work for us. He told us an
interesting story. He said right after he was President he went fishing
up in Canada. He went to the hotel in a little town, signed his name
Herbert Hoover, so and so address, U.S.A. The young man clerk there
got excited and said, ''Oooh, Herbert Hoover, by any chance are you
related to that famous American J. Edgar Hoover?'' So President
Hoover said he didn't crack a smile, he said, ''Oh, I've heard of him,
but I don't think we're related.'' Well, the young fellow thought for a
minute and said, ''Oh, by any chance are you related to the Hoover
vacuum people in the United States?'' Well, Mr. Hoover said he
hesitated a moment and then said, ''No, I don't believe they're related
to me.'' So the young man said, ''Well, no harm; up here in Canada

we get a kick out of entertaining people who have famous relatives.'' Mr. Hoover went fishing for a week and they never did know who he was.

Well, the most human of all the group, and I studied them from George Washington down, was President Truman, a real human, honest, down-to-earth man. He used to tell me, "Don't worry about criticism, history will take care of us." And before he died I saw him one day and I said, "Mr. President, you know they're already talking about you being a great President." "Well," he said, "that kind of surprises me, but," he said, "I didn't worry. If you do the right thing, history will take care of it." So he was a very human sort of fellow. I thought I'd give you one or two examples to stress the idea of his being human.

One time, again, we were down in Key West. The President and I were sitting on a bench under some coconut trees and a coconut fell and hit the bench right beside President Truman and it sounded like a cannon going off. The Secret Service agents got very excited and said, "Mr. President, you can't sit here any more." All the staff loved Truman so he could talk with them in a way that coming from some other President would have hurt their feelings. He said to the Secret Service agent, "What did you say?" "You can't sit here any more, Mr. President." Truman said, "Wait a minute, let's just see now. What are your duties?" He said, "My duties are to protect the President, that's why you can't sit here." Truman said, "Why don't we have an understanding along this line? You do your duty and I'll do mine, and we'll see how it works out." Next morning at breakfast we looked out towards the coconut trees and we saw one of the little Filipino sailors climbing up the coconut tree. He looked like a monkey; he was going up to examine all the coconuts to see if there were any that might fall that day. The Secret Service agents loved him, but they weren't telling him where he could sit. With a smile he said, "I'll sit where I please. Your job is to protect me, so protect me."

Another one: Admiral Leahy was Truman's military adviser. He inherited him from FDR and kept him a long time. At Key West the President, Admiral Leahy, and I lived in the so-called Little White House and the rest of the staff lived somewhere else, so we'd have breakfast together every morning at about seven o'clock. One morning at breakfast Admiral Leahy criticized one of the little sailors of the presidential yacht for feeding us too much of everything. Here sits President Truman, they take his order; they take my order; they come over to the admiral, who says, "Bacon, eggs, juice, so on and so forth, and *three* prunes." So the sailor comes in and he waits on us, and he started to walk off and sure enough he had given the admiral three prunes. Admiral Leahy said, "Come back here, boy." Truman said, "Wait a minute, Admiral. I'm commander in chief of the armed forces and that boy isn't afraid of me. He likes me and I like him. He's a human being just like you and me, but he's scared to death of you because you're an admiral." He said, "I heard you tell him three, you eat the three and don't you ever say a word to that boy." Well, the admiral said, "He ought to know I meant a small dish." Truman said, "Well, say small dish, don't tell him three and then criticize him for doing what you ordered." The admiral, you can be sure, never said a word to the sailor.

I'll give one other illustration. Truman demoted me once. We were playing poker and I accidentally beat him out of an $80 pot. I'm raking in the chips with glee, and he looked up and said, "John, what was your title when you left Washington day before yesterday?" I said, "Mr. President, you ought to know, you are the one who gave it to me." He said, "It slipped my mind, just what was it?" I said, "I'll have you know I'm the number two man in the government; I'm next to the President and my title is the assistant to the President of the United States." He said, "That's what you think. From now on you're chief file clerk in the White House." I'll mention later on in my talk how he came to put me back in my original position, but that was my title for the next several days.

Another little instance indicating Truman was human. Some writer was working on a book or an article on what do Presidents do when they step down from that lofty office. What do you do that first day you're home? So he asked President Truman. He thought a few moments and said, "Let's see, what did I do the first day? Oh, I know, I took all the suitcases up to the attic."

President Truman was not only human but he was an ethical man; he wanted things done right. Dr. Robert Turner, head of the School of Business Administration at Indiana University, used to be one of my assistants in the White House. He was a young economist who worked for me. During the time that Mr. Nixon was being criticized for a few things, Turner sent a Christmas card and he wrote a note on it, "You won't remember this, it didn't mean anything to you to see the President, as you saw him all the time. But once you took me with you to see President Truman. You had had me look up some information about a tariff problem between the United States and Switzerland. You took me with you (I used to take some of the staff members along occasionally because they liked to see the President), you let me explain the problem." And he said, "You know, after you and I had talked to the President about the tariff problem for about ten minutes the President spoke up and said, 'Look fellows, I don't know anything about the tariff situation, that's your job. I've just got one question to ask you: Is what you propose to do about this right?' " I said, "Mr. President, we're sure it is, we've studied it very carefully." He said, "Well, do it; good day." Turner said at the bottom of his note, "I don't hear any discussions about what's right around the White House any more."

President Truman, for relaxation, played poker. I only played with him at Key West once or twice a year, but he played nearly every Saturday night. He would play with some of his pals: former senators, former White House people, and so forth. Every Monday morning he'd say, "John, have you heard of such and such a case," some big issue up for decision; and I'd say, "Oh, yes, Mr. President, everybody in town is on one side or the other of that one." He'd say, "You better watch it. So and so mentioned it to me Saturday night when we were playing poker and he shouldn't have done it." Nobody could influence the President in that way. Among his poker-playing pals, there was one former senator that he was very fond of, and this senator knew you don't influence President Truman. The senator would come down and chew the rag with Truman, oh I'd say every two or three months. They'd have a nice little conversation, sometimes I'd go in with him. On the way out the senator would stop at the door and say, "By the way, Mr. President, I promised a friend of mine I'd mention this case so and so to you," Truman would say, "Fine, fine, you mentioned it, good day." Truman would say, "He probably got five or ten for that, but you better watch it, John, there must be something wrong with it or they wouldn't have hired him to see me."

So whatever anybody ever tells you, I happen to know he was an honest, straightforward, ethical man. He gave his mother credit. She taught him to do right. He said his mother used to say, "Harry can plow the straightest row of anybody in the state of Missouri and whatever else he does he does it just right, just straight," Truman and Lincoln both gave their mothers credit. Lincoln said, "All that I am or ever expect to be, I give the credit to my mother." George Washington never mentioned his mother in that way.

I'll give you one other example of Truman's honesty. One day a group of people, a small group were having lunch in New York. Among them was a Boston lawyer who happened to know me, and knew a little more about how we worked at the White House. These fellows were talking, and one of them said he had a million dollar case against the government—some contract or something—that he ran into a Washington lobbyist who was a very close friend of Truman's, or had been, and the lobbyist had said he thought he could handle it for us. He'd handle it for $25,000, and we thought well, $25,000 versus a million, it's a good gamble, we'll hire him. The lobbyist had said, "Fifteen down and ten if I win it for you." Well, this lawyer heard them talking and he said, "Gentlemen, in the first place he couldn't influence Truman anyhow but I doubt that Truman ever heard of your case." He said, "John Steelman wouldn't have sent a thing like that to the President; he probably handled it himself. I bet Truman never heard of it, and I'll tell you how you can find out. John's left the government but he's still in Washington. If you want to find out the truth just go down and have lunch with John and ask him about the case." So he called me and made a date with this fellow to have lunch with me. The fellow told me the whole situation and asked me, "Did the President handle that or did you?" and I said, "Oh, the President never handled it, I wouldn't bother him with that; I handled it." I said, "You lost. I was right, wasn't I?" and the guy said, "Yes, to tell you the truth you were. But," he said, "we thought it was a good bet, 25 against a million." And he said, "Did this fellow ever mention the case to you or the President?" and I said, "No. He'd know better than mention it to me and if he had mentioned it to the President, the President would have tipped me off to watch it." He said, "In other words we got 'took' for fifteen and if by accident you would have ruled in our favor, ten more." I said, "That's right." So that's the way it goes. Well, anyway, that's enough about Truman being honest.

I want to mention another thing that hasn't been publicized much, and that was his education. He never went to college, but I have worked with and under and above numerous Ph.D.s and I never yet worked with anybody who was better educated than Truman. That sounds like a big statement and I'll tell you why. All his life he was a great reader, read everything. But I could do that and it wouldn't mean much. Truman had nearest to a perfect photographic memory of anybody I've ever seen. I've met three in my life who had that knack. He could turn the pages of a book and tomorrow or ten years from tomorrow he could tell you what page, what line, what paragraph a statement was in. It's hard to believe the way he could tell you, what page and what line a statement was on when he probably hadn't seen it for ten years. I can't do that; I wish I could. No wonder he was a great President. So the fact that he didn't go to college, don't let it fool you. He was a well educated man.

A problem would arise and he'd say, "Why, they had that in ancient history. The Romans had it; the Greeks had it." He'd tell you how each one had it, what the problem was and so forth. He'd go right back to the beginning of history and tell you how every issue of that kind had come up and how they handled it. So he was better educated than the public has ever realized, and that's the reason. As I say, I've met two others like that in my life. I met a man at Harvard University who could do that, and strange to say, you wouldn't guess who the third one was; it was John L. Lewis, president of the United Mine Workers' Union. Lewis could quote the Bible from the first to the last word; he could quote every Shakespeare play ever written; and he never went to college, but he had that memory. A group of coal operators got me to go over with them once to see John Lewis about shipping coal to South America after the war because they said South America was going to be industrialized. Lewis said, "Why, gentlemen, that's not true." He said, "In South America they are not going to have any industrial revolution. To have an industrial nation you have to give the workers enough money to buy back what they make." He said, "They're not about to do that in South America while you and I live. Ninety-eight percent is owned by two percent," and so forth. So he said, "Look at their budgets, " and he told us, he started with Central America and he went down through every country in South America. He quoted their budget; where the money comes from; and how it is spent. These coal operators sat there with their mouths open. And then Lewis said, "Gentlemen, let's look at Europe, that's where the industrial developments are going to be after the war," and he gave us the budget of all the European countries. One of the coal men said, "John, how on earth do you know this stuff?" and he said, "Well, you birds have always expected me to know these things. I get these budgets and look them over." He looks them over and he can tell you every word that's in them.

I don't know if you've met that kind of person. As I've said, I've met three in my life and Truman was one of them. So he was better educated than the public ever realized. He knew the history of the world like all the history professors combined. Truman knew it all because he had read it and he'd never forgotten, he could still see it. So he was a well educated man as well as human and an honest one.

Now I want to stress a quality that I suspect others have stressed—that he was an excellent administrator. That's what his job really was, after all.

President Roosevelt wasn't very strong on administration; he was the greatest politician I ever saw, but he wasn't as good an administrator as President Truman. President Truman knew how to delegate and when he delegated he delegated. He was like old

Chancellor Kirkland at Vanderbilt when I was a graduate student. He said, "Now Mr. Steelman, you're in charge of the dormitories. So why should I worry about the dormitories? I don't even know they're here." He said, "I'm careful who I hire as head of my history department but after that I forget there is a history department. No use in both of us worrying about it." He used to be a professor of botany with 30 students and all at once he was a big university chancellor. I asked him how he did the job without worrying. He said, "I really have nothing to do. Everything here is somebody else's job." He said, "You go in my office you probably wouldn't see a piece of paper on my desk." He said, "Every once in a while my secretary brings me something to sign but outside of that I really don't have anything to do because everything is delegated.

So he taught me how to appreciate President Truman when the time came. Anyway, President Truman, not long after I went with him, called me in and said, "John, I want to say a few things to you in confidence." The subject arose about somebody from New England. He said, "John, he doesn't really understand America like you and I do, you know the soil we came out of." He made a great to-do, about the heart of America. "I'm from Missouri and you're from Arkansas, we understand each other." He said, "I know what you're going to say before you say it or what you're going to decide and you know me in the same way. So take part of this load and don't even tell me about it, just do it." He said, "There's too much here for one person," but he thought because we were from the same region, the "heart of the country," that we understood each other better. Maybe we did, but he made a great to-do about our being from "the center" of America.

He told me to do things and not even tell him unless I wanted to. I remember one time he had given me a tough assignment in connection with the economy. I found it necessary to fire the chairman of the Federal Reserve. I doubt if the President could get away with that today. So I went in to see President Truman and said, "Mr. President, I just did a terrible thing," and he said, "What's that?" and I said, "I fired the chairman of the Federal Reserve Board," and he said, "What did you do a thing like that for?" I said, "Well, he wouldn't cooperate with me on a job you gave me to do." "Oh," he said, "in that event leave him fired."

One time the president of an oil company was called in by President Truman and asked if he'd serve on an advisory committee on oil problems. The President asked him if he would serve and he said he would, so he said, "Well, see John Steelman, he'll tell you what to do." I was very busy and the man kept calling my secretary for an appointment. Finally, about four o'clock in the afternoon he told her what he ought to have in the first place; that he had seen the President and the President wanted him to see me. I was across the street; the President often gave me two or three other jobs besides my regular one. If we had an important vacancy come up, he'd say, "I'm going to tell the press you're it, until you find somebody." So I was across the street acting as chairman of the National Security Resources Board. So about four o'clock the man tells my secretary he can't go home until he sees me. She called me and explained. I said, "How does my calendar look?" She said, "Well, your last appointment is twelve o'clock tonight." I said, "Well, switch him over, I'll talk to him." I said, "I can see you at 12:15 tonight or 7, 8, 9, 10 tomorrow. What do you prefer?" "Oh," he said, "I can't go home until I see you. I'll see you tonight." He came over to the White House, and sat with me for an hour. At about 1:15, we had talked I suppose five to ten minutes during the time. He said, "Do you realize how many people you've talked to tonight—how many Cabinet officers and departmental heads and so forth?" and I said, "No, I've been too busy to keep count." He said, "You've talked to seven Cabinet officers about problems all over the world and you've talked to three other independent agency heads about problems." He said, "If my mother had told me what I've heard here I would not have believed her. I'm glad I didn't see you till midnight. I'm one of these businessmen who go around saying government people don't work." I said, "Now don't be fooled by that, they don't all work quite this late. The higher up you get the harder you have to work." Well, anyhow, he said, "I wouldn't even have believed my mother." The point is that the President turned many problems over to me. I was there so I could take part of the load.

To go back a bit, the President called me on one day and showed me a memorandum that some Cabinet officers had written. They had been to a meeting down in Hot Springs, Virginia with a group of corporation heads and they were getting ready for the greatest depression in history. Remember for every war there is a depression, they said, therefore after the greatest war, look out for the greatest depression. And they were warning the President to get ready. The President called me in and he was kind of grinning and he said, "John, didn't you study economics at Harvard?" and he said, "You know I never went to college." I said, "Yes, Mr. President, I studied there on a scholarship but I didn't learn much. The only economics I know is what an old gray-headed professor down in Arkansas told me once. 'Forget all the theories and remember this: economics is just plain horse sense.'" I said, "Mr. President, my plain horse sense, what little I have, tells me we ought to have a boom not a depression. The shelves are all empty, you can't buy anything. All we need to do is get to work," and Truman typically pointed his finger and said, "You see that we do not have a depression. If I can ever be of assistance call on me." He used to say he looked for easy ones to give me.

I had to do quite a few things. Everything I had to do hit somebody. For example I held up $9 billion of public works money. I issued an order—"None of this shall be spent until I say so." Well, Mr. Nixon tried that in later years, before Watergate, and practically got run out of town. I believe Congress passed a law, I don't believe even the President today could do what I did, but back in those days it was a little indefinite and the senators and congressmen were all friends of mine anyway, so they didn't criticize me. Some Cabinet officers said, "Mr. President, you'll have to overrule John, he has no right to do this, he's going to throw a lot of people out of work." Well, that's just what I wanted to do because I wanted them to go right over into the factories. Let the public works go awhile. So they said, "You'll have to overrule John." Truman said, "I'm sorry, I can't mention it to him." They said, "Can't mention it to him? Aren't you the boss around here?" Truman said, "Yes, I'm the boss in general but John issued that order as I understand it in connection with an assignment I gave him, we had an understanding that he could call me if he needed me, I can't call him." That was that. So when he delegated, he delegated.

Another illustration—I told you the President demoted me for winning his money in a poker game one night. Well, we got back to Washington and a day or two later he called me in and said, "I've got to reinstate you. I have something for you to do that a file clerk couldn't handle." I said, "I'm sure glad to get my job back, but Mr. President, what do you want me to do now?" and he said, "I've learned from the secretary of state and from the cloak and dagger boys (this was before we had CIA) that the government of Italy is about to fall, about to fall to Communism." He said, "Now if that happens the Communists take the whole of Europe within thirty days or we'll find ourselves right back into World War III." He said, "You know I'm President," and I said "Yes, Mr. President, I've heard that." He said, "I remind you I'm also commander in chief of the armed forces," and I said "Yes, Mr. President, I've heard that, too." He said, "In both capacities I place myself at your command. You see that Italy does not fall." Out I go again, wondering what do I do now. Well, I had to do some unpopular things again. The trouble was similar to what we had experienced here. In Italy they needed to get to work. It's hard to shift over suddenly from war production to civilian production. I had to send some scrap iron over to Italy. I called the experts in to see what the trouble was. For one thing they said, "The steel mills are not operating, Italy is short on scrap iron." I said, "Why don't they go out in the battlefield and pick up some? There must be plenty of that around Italy." Well, it wasn't quite so simple. We had to send some over. Typically I tried not to pull surprises on people, so I sent for the presidents of the steel companies and I said, "Fellows, I must do something you aren't going to like, we've been friends for years, I've settled your strikes for you, and so forth. Now I've got to do something you won't like, and you criticize me publicly all you please but just let's still be friends." I'll never forget Ben Fairless of U.S. Steel. He said, "John, if you have to do it, you have to do it, go ahead. We'll understand." Soon criticism filled the air, the steel workers in Pittsburgh were going to be thrown out of jobs. Finally, some staff members went to Truman. They said, "Mr. President, you have to overrule John. Next year's election is coming up and the people in Rome aren't going to vote, the people John threw out of work in Pittsburgh will vote and you know how." Truman again said, "I'm sorry, I can't mention that subject to John. I had an understanding with him, if he needs me he can call me, I can't call him." So again when he delegated, he delegated. He was a real administrator.

I'll mention one other example. I refer to the Berlin airlift. Truman called me late at night and said, "John, something has happened, it won't wait till Monday." This was Saturday night. He said, "We better have a meeting tomorrow, Sunday, two o'clock. Get the Cabinet there and get the leaders from the Hill there. We've got a serious problem." I didn't know what he was talking about. At the meeting he told us about Russia blockading West Berlin. So we discussed the various alternatives: what will happen if we don't do anything? "Well, they'll take Europe," said the secretary of state. Truman asked the secretary of defense, "Are we ready to blast them at six o'clock in the morning?" Well, the secretary of defense said, "We're not in very good shape for that, Mr. President. We'd better find another way if we can." Truman turned to the secretary of the Air Force and said, "Are you prepared, starting at six in the morning, to fly wheat, coal, produce, whatever they need into West Berlin, to fly it in there?" The secretary squirmed and said, "Mr. President, I don't see how we could do it that quickly." Truman said, "We have eliminated the other alternatives, so do it. . . . The meeting is adjourned." I'll never forget Charlie Halleck, Republican leader of the House, who waited in the hall for me. As we walked down the hall together and he said, "Gosh,

John, what a man you work for. In my position I'll probably have to criticize him before sundown tomorrow but if I do, remember this, I don't mean a word of it." He admired Truman for his decisiveness.

I've said enough. I just wanted to stress the human part of Truman, the honesty part of him. I wanted to discuss him as a better educated man than has been realized, and lastly, as a real administrator. After all that's what the job calls for. No one person can do that job alone any more, and so you have to get a good staff and depend on them. He was careful about that and he did it. So that's about enough, those are the points I wanted to stress, and I know you may have some questions.

MR. THOMPSON: Three people who delegate to me on occasion are here and I am especially pleased that they are: Jack Hancock is a member of the governing Council of the Miller Center and a leading industrialist from Roanoke. Many of you have known and respected him over the years. And Wilson Newman at the far end of the table, the former chairman and chief executive officer of Dun and Bradstreet, who is now a resident on Charlottesville, is also here and is a member of our governing Council. We're also pleased to have a member of our University Board of Visitors here, Dr. Edgar Weaver, the top neurosurgeon in the state. Who'd like to ask the first question?

QUESTION: I always admired Truman very much when he was President, Mr. Steelman, and I must say I was very disappointed at him as an ex-President. It seemed to me he was a much less sensitive, a much less cautious person in what he said. It struck me that he was a man maybe like Al Smith who flowered when he had responsibilities, but was not the same man when he didn't have responsibilities. Is that too harsh a thought? Did I misread him when he left the presidency?

MR. STEELMAN: I'm not sure. I think that may be true. His idea was, when you're through, you're through, therefore you can do what you please. I think he probably wasn't quite as careful as he might have been sometimes. I wasn't in very close touch with him afterwards. I did see him a few times but there is something to what you say, I'm sure. I hadn't thought it until you mentioned it.

QUESTION: What was the reason he chose to back Harriman as his successor rather than Stevenson in 1952?

MR. STEELMAN: First of all, he was very fond of Harriman, but mainly, I don't know how to put it, he liked Stevenson but he said, "He'll never go over with the public. He is a little too sophisticated for the general public; he couldn't possibly win." So I think that was the main reason, plus the fact that he was very close to Harriman.

QUESTION: Did you have any personal observations to add with respect to the termination of the relationship between the President and General MacArthur?

MR. STEELMAN: Nothing in particular. Long after Truman fired MacArthur he said he was probably the greatest general we ever had. The trouble with Mr. MacArthur was that he couldn't adjust to peacetime, he couldn't be a part of the global strategy that we had to work with. He kept getting out of line making statements that were contrary to overall policy and so forth, and finally one after another recommended to Truman to let him go, and Truman was very hesitant to do so. General Marshall was the last holdout. He said, "Mr. President, maybe we can work it out with him, maybe we can get him to understand." Truman finally went to see him. He met the general and explained things to him. The general said he understood and that he would cooperate; that he wouldn't make statements about policy without clearing them. And about two weeks later he broke out again and General Marshall, the last holdout, came and said, "Mr. President, you've been right all along. We'll have to let him go." He just didn't adjust to peacetime. He was a great general, no doubt about that. By the way, his wife still lives in the Waldorf Towers in New York. She's still there. She was much younger than he.

QUESTION: Mr. Steelman, there are quite a number of people who express concern that President Truman didn't understand the significance of Eastern Europe. They say it was a kind of omission that Eastern Europe unnecessarily went under the Soviet umbrella, and that, as the workshop in the intervening years since it is really the industrial backbone of the Soviet Union. My question is: Are you aware whether President Truman felt constrained to keep hands off the Eastern European problem? Was he precommitted to let Eastern Europe go behind the Iron Curtain?

MR. STEELMAN: I'm not sure, to be honest with you, what the answer to that is.

QUESTION: It's turned out to be a testing ground for national resolve from the standpoint of the United States. It had the industrial muscle, and the technology for defense that the Russians have comes out of Czechoslovakia and the other countries.

QUESTION: Do you know why FDR thought Truman would be his most appropriate successor?

MR. STEELMAN: I think I do. The general feeling was that the vice president would be either Jimmy Byrnes or Henry A. Wallace.

Roosevelt had purposely or inadvertently led each one of them to think he was the next vice presidential candidate and everybody knew that meant the next President. The President himself knew he wouldn't live it out and everybody else did. So the best I can tell you is that FDR, knowing both of these gentlemen better than anybody else probably, didn't think either one of them was presidential timber, that either of them would fit as President in the postwar period. Truman, whom he had come to know through his work on the Truman Committee on the Hill (the senatorial committee interested in war production), had impressed FDR as the one who would be a better President than either one of those two for the postwar period.

QUESTION: Was FDR unusual in that opinion? Was that the view of other knowledgeable people in the government?

MR. STEELMAN: The only thing anybody knew about Senator Truman was his work on the Truman Committee, the senatorial committee interested in war production, and I think the general opinion at the time was that they didn't think too much about the vice presidency. If you'd ask the general population I think they probably would have said Truman was not big enough for the job. That was a kind of a general impression. After all he had been a haberdasher who failed in business. The critics didn't know him, but FDR knew him and decided he ought to be the next President.

QUESTION: I am under the impression that of all the executives in the government at that time, he was probably the only one who thought that.

MR. STEELMAN: The President was? That may well be, or at least maybe he thought that most. That may be.

QUESTION: On the basis of President Truman seizing the steel mills, did he do that under a kind of a war measures act or was it that there was a critical shortage of steel at that time? Was that really necessary? Did he have any second thoughts?

MR. STEELMAN: No, I don't think so. I was into that and they weren't very close to an agreement. All the information we could get was that we couldn't stand the strike. Maybe we could have; it depended on how long it lasted, of course. But he did it, he thought at least, in the interest of the country.

QUESTION: You indicated that the decision process of President Truman with respect to General MacArthur involved some collegial assistance in discussion with those around him. I think one generally gets the impression that he was accused at the time of shooting from the hip, yet he had uncanny accuracy in the shots. My question is: Was collegial participation important in reaching the decision with respect to the Hiroshima bomb?

MR. STEELMAN: That happened just before I went with the President, but yes, my impression is, and I've heard it discussed many times, it was very thoroughly discussed and it finally came down to where he was convinced that it was 250,000 to 300,000 of our young men or drop the bomb. And on any decision he made he'd get all the information he could from everybody concerned. He had a knack for making the decision then and he could go home and go to sleep. I couldn't if I made that decision but he could. So I'm sure he got all the information he could. In other words, the only way you can lick Japan is to go in and take it; we're not about to give up. And it was just our men or them, it was what it boiled down to.

May I tell you about a strange little incident? I used to play golf with a Japanese ambassador out at Burning Tree Golf Club. One day he and I were partners and we were beginning to win, and I said, "Ambassador, you know I like you a lot better now than I did a few years ago." He said, "John, if you and I had been in charge that never would have happened." He said, "The military got control of our government and got us into something that we couldn't possibly win." He said, "It was a great tragedy. If you and I had been in power we'd have settled it, you know, amicably, but the military got us into it."

QUESTION: It sounds as if you had done a lot of work while Mr. Truman had the leisure to read.

MR. STEELMAN: No, he worked as hard as I did except he didn't work the hours I did. I got the habit under President Roosevelt of not sleeping. So when I went with President Truman it was the same. He'd already done his reading before he got to the White House. He'd read almost everything that had ever been printed, I think, but he still was a reader. And he worked as hard as I did except not as many hours. When he'd get ready to go to bed he could see my office from his bedroom window. I had an understanding with his secretary when the President called me late at night I knew he was going to bawl me out about working and so she and I had a certain little ring she'd give me and I'd know it was the President calling, so I'd wait about a minute and I'd answer, and he'd get on the phone and he'd say, "What are you doing down there this time of night?" and I'd say, "Oh, Mr.

President, I'm glad I came back, I was just going down the hall getting ready to go home and I heard the phone ringing. I'm glad I came back." He'd say, "Why don't you go on home?" so I'd say, "I'm just ready to go" and then he'd go to sleep and I'd work to five o'clock, maybe, if I had to. Yes, he still read a lot but he worked, too. He didn't take it easy.

MR. THOMPSON: We're terribly grateful to you for opening new windows on Mr. Truman as a person and as a leader. We hope since you come up here from points south from time to time that you will visit the Miller Center again and talk about other subjects.

MR. STEELMAN: I've learned a thing or two. Two or three of you have raised questions that I hadn't thought of. It's good to get groups like this together. That's your idea to get the whole truth out. Very interesting. Glad to see you all.

PERSONNEL FOR THE TRUMAN WHITE HOUSE
Ken Hechler

MR. THOMPSON: We are pleased to have with us at one of the Forums on the Truman presidency Ken Hechler of West Virginia. His presence is very timely, as he has just published a book called *Working With Truman: A Personal Memoir of the White House Years.*

Ken Hechler is a Democrat from Huntington, West Virginia. He served in the Congress for nine terms and in the Truman White House as a special assistant to President Truman. Some of you knew that he was the author of *The Bridge at Remagen,* the account of the first Rhine crossing in World War II which became a motion picture released by United Artists in 1969. He is also the author of *Insurgency: Personalities and Politics of the Taft Era, Toward the Endless Frontier,* and *West Virginia Memories of President Kennedy.* He has served as associate executive director of the American Political Science Association.

His government service is equally strong in both the executive branch and the legislative branch. He was personnel officer of the Office for Emergency Management in 1941; section chief in the Bureau of the Census; administrative analyst in the Bureau of the Budget in

1942 and again from 1946 to 1947. He served with great distinction in the United States Army enlisting as a private, commissioned second lieutenant of the Armored Forces in 1943; assigned to ETO as combat historian in 1944; received five battle stars from Normandy to the Elbe; participated in the interrogation of Hermann Goering and other top German military leaders; was discharged as major and obviously in that capacity prepared, among other things the Remagen bridge account.

It is a great pleasure to include in our Truman presidency series a discussion by Ken Hechler on the Truman White House, particularly the staffing of the White House and any related issues he may want to introduce.

MR. HECHLER: Thank you. It is an honor to be here at the Miller Center. The news media are filled every day with items that remind you of Harry Truman. On Saturday I was reading that President Reagan had made a surprise visit to his senior staff meeting. This was labeled as "unprecedented." It was almost as though an intruder had come in and you wondered whether Mr. Baker and Mr. Meese had asked for his security clearance. What a contrast with Harry Truman who always conducted personally his own staff meetings. Every morning at 9:30 he would get the senior staff together in a semi-circle around his desk. Matt Connelly, the appointment secretary, would start off with a discussion of the appointments of the day and what was coming up in the next few weeks and then each member of the staff would have an opportunity to bring up what was on his mind, interspersed by comments from President Truman. There was never any doubt who was in charge.

After the staff meeting and after his regular appointments he would sometimes stick his head into offices of various members to see how things were going. He did this not to prod or interfere or, as President Johnson would do, saying: "I assigned you this at 3:30, here it is 4:00. Why don't you have it?" It was rather to offer additional advice or input to the White House staff.

Any President who is elected to office and has several months of *interregnum* has an opportunity to cross-check the competence of those who are going to work for him, to have a transition team meeting with counterparts of the outgoing administration, and to decide on the structure and operating relationships of the new White House staff before the baton is passed on the 20th of January. Late in the afternoon of April 12, 1945 when Vice President Truman received the shocking news from Eleanor Roosevelt that her husband had died at Warm Springs, he convened a Cabinet meeting within two hours, after which Secretary of War Henry Stimson stayed behind to inform him of the development of an explosive with unbelievable destructive power. That was the first news that Harry Truman had heard about the atom bomb. He was faced immediately, without even an opportunity to wait over night, with the necessity to select a staff, to pick a Cabinet, deciding which of the Roosevelt holdovers were so devoted to FDR that they could not carry on under a new President, and thinking about what kind of an organization his White House staff should have.

I think he was handicapped even more by his relationship with Roosevelt. In the eighty-three days that he had been vice president he had seen Roosevelt alone only twice and he had no briefing on the subtleties of the change in the attitude of the Soviet Union and the challenges posed by rapidly moving international events. I've had a lot of arguments with the Carter White House staff and other White House staffs about the small size of the Truman staff. They frequently contend that the problems today are so much more complex than in Harry Truman's time. Well, I don't want to list all the problems but all you have to do is recall that although the war was practically won in Europe, we still faced heavy fighting in the Far East. Ahead of us was demobilization and reconversion, and the eruption of strikes all over the country as labor attemped to get out from under the ceilings imposed during the World War II controls. There was the problem of international control, nuclear weapons, the delicate issues involved in establishing the United Nations and other international bodies in the face of Russian intransigence and aggressive expansion. Then there was the collapse of Chiang Kai-Shek, the defeat of the French in Indochina, the eruption of the war in Korea, and the problems of inflation and stabilization of the economy. You name it. The world was in turmoil and there was war in the Middle East with the creation of the new state of Israel in 1948. Russian troops were remaining in Iran after World War II. Tito was threatening Trieste. Well, I could go on for a long time. I don't think the problems were less complex in Harry Truman's time. So I think the question of the size of the White House staff remains a crucial one because it is related to the ability of the President to control and command his own White House operation.

Some of the Carter staff argued with me that there are so many different minority groups now that you need an assistant for all shades of opinion and group organization. Of course, when you set up so many assistants in the White House it almost forces them to be advocates of each group and it's difficult to maintain leadership and breadth of perspective.

The relationship with Roosevelt of course also was marred somewhat by the fact that Roosevelt initially had a favorite candidate for the U.S. Senate (Missouri Governor Lloyd Stark) in 1940 when

Truman ran for reelection. Roosevelt initially wanted to appoint Senator Truman to the Interstate Commerce Commission to get him out of the way so that his favorite candidate could win.

Although a very strong supporter of the New Deal and an admirer of Roosevelt as a great national and world leader, Truman was quite suspicious of some of the people that he called "the crackpots," meaning people like Henry Wallace in the Roosevelt orbit.

I recall very vividly a meeting with President Truman the day after he publicly announced at the 1952 Jefferson-Jackson Day Dinner on March 29 his decision not to run for reelection. We were sitting around the table in the Cabinet Room, and the President spoke of how important it was to plan for the next administration.

Personally, my thoughts were zeroed in on trying to make sure that there would be a Democrat in the White House, but quite typically Harry Truman was looking farther into the future. He said we should start right away to set down on paper how we could insure a smooth transition, whether the next President was a Republican or a Democrat. He underlined the fact that when he had become President, he did not have this kind of briefing, and he wanted to be sure that the next President would not be handicapped the way he had been. You could tell from the emotion and determination in his voice that he felt very strongly about Roosevelt's failure to give him any idea of the nature of the problems pending, or the organization of the staff to help to meet these problems.

Truman's two immediate sources of White House staff personnel were the Roosevelt holdovers and some of his Capitol Hill staff as vice president and senator as well as people that he knew and trusted in Missouri. There were problems with both groups. Many Roosevelt assistants just couldn't cotton to the idea of Harry Truman carrying on in the Roosevelt tradition. One exception was Judge Samuel I. Rosenman who had been Roosevelt's special counselor since the time he was governor in New York and who remained loyally as Truman's special counsel and chief speechwriter until February 1946, and afterward on an informal basis. In fact, the close personal friendship with Rosenman lasted until Truman's death. Judge and Mrs. Rosenman also accompanied the Trumans to France and Italy in a trip after President Truman had left the White House.

Tall, erudite and personable William D. Hassett, a Vermonter whose prose could soothe raging beasts, stayed on as Correspondence Secretary until his declining health forced him to retire in 1952. Another loyal Roosevelt holdover, mystery man David K. Niles, once described as a "portable wailing wall" for minority groups, stayed on with his assistant, Philleo Nash who suceeded him after Niles died in 1951. Most of Roosevelt's administrative assistants left rather quickly, as did Roosevelt's naval aide, Vice Admiral Wison Brown, who stayed only a month until the arrival of Missouri friend Commodore James K. Vardaman, Jr., who proved to be an example of a Truman assistant who contracted "Potomac Fever" and was shunted over to the Federal Reserve Board after less than a year.

There were several other exceptions: Steve Early and Jonathan Daniels in the Roosevelt press office were extremely helpful in the transition period before Truman was able to get his old Missouri classmate and valedictorian of the Independence High School class, Charles G. Ross, to come in as press secretary. Ross was one of the Missourians who was really outstanding. Their long friendship enabled a close rapport between the two individuals and Ross was an excellent spokesman to the press and to the people about Truman policies. Ross was also one of the key advisers to Truman and a force for liberalism in the struggles that went on between the east wing of the White House and the west wing. East is east and west is west. And the twain sometimes didn't meet. The east wing was largely controlled by John Steelman, whose title was the assistant to the President. He had as his general allies John Snyder, the secretary of the treasury, Matt Connelly, the appointment secretary, and a number of others in the government who were constantly struggling with the west wing group which was headed by Clark Clifford, the special counsel, and his staff. I was part of this group of liberal agitators who were always talking out in favor of more advanced policies. When I say liberalism I mean national health insurance, civil rights, housing, the Point Four Program as opposed to massive capital expenditures, holding the line against anti-labor legislation, and also strongly supporting President Truman's veto of a Republican-sponsored tax bill which was very similar to a Reagan tax bill tilted in favor of the more wealthy classes of the country.

My major criticism of President Truman was one of the so-called "Missouri gang" that he kept far longer than he should have and that was his military aide, General Harry Hawkins Vaughan. He was somewhat of a buffoon, a very fast man on his feet who performed the function of court jester and was able to help Truman relieve some of the crushing burdens of the presidency by a joke at the right time. He was really funny. This is no excuse for some of the trouble he got President Truman in but he was really hilarious. For example, one day Dean Acheson had made a great speech, and I was bragging about it to General Vaughan over lunch at the White House. I noted that Acheson had ended that speech with a moving plea for "the peace that passeth all understanding." General Vaughan chomped on his cigar, poked me in the ribs and answered: "You know, Dean would get along a lot better if he'd pay less attention to the Sermon on the Mount and more to the men on the Hill."

As you cross Arlington Memorial bridge by the Lincoln Memorial there are four statues of horses that are painted so they gleam with a golden hue. They were donated by the government of Italy in appreciation for our post-World War II aid and President Truman went out with Premier deGasperi to dedicate those statues. As we came up to the statues we saw they were draped with canvas and there was a long thin rope attached to them, which President Truman was supposed to pull to unveil the statues. He turned to General Vaughan and he said, "Harry, what should I say when I pull that string?" Vaughan right quick snapped back, "That's easy, boss, all you say is 'They're off'!'"

Despite these humorous sallies which relieved some of the tension around the White House, Harry Vaughan was like a friendly puppy dog to all kinds of self-seekers. He'd invite lobbyists, outside interests, and those anxious to get something out of the White House. Then they would get Truman into trouble by bragging they had an inside track to the White House. I'm certain that the Republicans got a lot of grist for their campaign mill in 1952—talking about Korea, corruption, and communism—charging that corruption was somehow connected with Harry Vaughan. The deep freezes that General Vaughan gave away were penny ante stuff contrasted to scandals in other administrations, but Vaughan hurt Truman.

Truman was never reluctant to fire other people on the White House staff that got out of line, but Vaughan was a big exception. Harry Vaughan had been with him in World War I, had been his finance manager in the crucial 1940 senatorial campaign and he was a great poker buddy. Out at the Truman Library there is a letter that the President wrote to Mrs. Truman, a copy of which I have here, wherein he relates how Vaughan rushed out to talk to the press while Truman, Ross and Steelman were preparing a careful public statement on the flood situation. When writing to Bess, Truman calls him "Mr. Malaprop." But he admits to Bess that he has to keep him. He writes: "My military aide doesn't know he's done wrong! I can't bring myself to pulverize him because he's been so mistreated I don't want to add to his unhappiness."

But there are some examples of others Truman wasn't reluctant to fire. Another World War I buddy named Edward McKim was brought in by President Truman and designated as chief administrative assistant in April 1945. McKim immediately got a big head. He began to draw boxes and charts and throw his weight around. This of course was contrary to the kind of pragmatic way in which President Truman liked to run his staff operation. Eddie McKim had his white tie and tails in the office constantly ready to step out. He got mesmerized by the social scene. I found a little note in one of President Truman's press conferences in June 13, 1945 and you can understand what this means even though it was said very nicely: "John Snyder put a draft on Ed McKim to get him away from me for a special job, and I guess I'll have to let him go for the time being." Well, he never returned to the White House staff. And there were several other cases of people who got what President Truman used to call "Potomac fever." He would quote Woodrow Wilson, that two things happened to people who came to Washington—"they either grow or they swell." Some people on the White House staff began to swell and when they did swell Harry Truman got rid of them. That he wasn't reluctant to do, although the retention of Vaughan is a special case.

Then there was the case of a good friend of mine, Stephen Spingarn. Steve was a mountain of a man who was a bachelor and loved his work so much he just never stopped. We would go down to Key West ostensibly to rest and Steve would be writing memos and be on the telephone while the rest of us were swimming or playing volleyball. His expertise was civil rights, civil liberties and he was such a passionate advocate of the Truman program that he would spend a lot of time on Capitol Hill propagandizing what Truman stood for. For some obscure reason nobody could ever fully understand, he went just a little too far in his insistence that Vice President Barkley should take a more aggressive position on a Truman issue, and the first thing we heard was that Barkley complained bitterly to the President about Spingarn. It was then announced that Spingarn had been elevated to fill a vacancy on the Federal Trade Commission. Spingarn tried desperately to argue the President out of it, but the President was firm.

There was some very able talent available to Harry Truman. In the crucial area of foreign policy he was fortunate to have Ambassador Averell Harriman, who was then in Moscow, fly back and help brief the President on emerging developments in foreign policy. Harriman came trotting in and was surprised to find that Truman had already read the full details of what had happened at Yalta, and had been briefed by Jimmy Byrnes who took stenographic notes of that conference. It came as a surprise to some of the White House staff that Truman didn't want one-page summaries like an unnamed successor to President Truman. He wanted the full details.

Harriman relates he once sent a report to Truman which had been prepared by one of his assistants, with a summary at the end and Harriman had only read the summary. He was very embarrassed to find that Truman was asking questions on the body of the report and Harriman said he never made the mistake again.

Harry Hopkins, even though he was very ill at the time was also able to brief President Truman on relations with Stalin. There was another able Roosevelt holdover, the chief of staff to the commander in chief, Fleet Admiral William D. Leahy who assisted on foreign policy, as did General George Marshall whose outlook extended far beyond the confines of the military.

There was also a young, twenty-four year old history major from Princeton University who got his masters degree in history at Harvard named George Elsey who was assigned as a naval ensign to the map room of the White House when Roosevelt was President. During that service in the map room Judge Rosenman frequently called on him for summaries of some of the military data in cables and other data. This proved to be very useful in the later work which Elsey did in speechwriting. Elsey became the assistant to Clark Clifford, and later an administrative assistant to the President. He was a key figure in the 1948 campaign in drafting the outlines for the great whistle-stop speeches which Truman made during the successful upset victory of 1948.

Elsey was a registered Republican when he was recruited. It's interesting that Harry Truman, a product of the Pendergast machine, had several people at the White House who had been registered Republicans. In fact, I have to confess that I was also registered as a Republican when I was recruited at the White House and nobody put a piece of litmus paper in my mouth to see what color it would come out. Press Secretary Roger Tubby had been a Vermont Republican, and saw the light later on.

Some of the greatest successes that Truman scored in foreign policy in 1947 and 1948 were due to the fact that he befriended Senator Arthur H. Vandenberg, the chairman of the Senate Foreign Relations Comittee, and was able to get the Republicans to believe he would be only a one-term President, therefore they might as well give him the Truman Doctrine, the Marshall Plan, NATO, the support of the Berlin airlift, and all the other great decisions that President Truman made to provide that shield for freedom in Western Europe.

One measure of the competence of the White House staff is in their subsequent careers. Clark Clifford, whom I mentioned, went on to become secretary of defense under President Johnson and now is one of the most successful lawyers in the nation's capital. There are many others that I should mention who are perhaps not as well known.

George Elsey went on to become national president of the American Red Cross, recently retired. Harold L. Enarson became president of Ohio State University, I'm sure not because of his White House connections but because of his sheer ability. David E. Bell became President Kennedy's budget director, headed the foreign aid program under President Johnson and was later executive vice president of the Ford Foundation. Roger Tubby became U.S. ambassador to the European office of the United Nations. Clayton Fritchey became a nationally-syndicated columnist. David Stowe became chairman of the National Mediation Board. Charles Murphy became under secretary of agriculture and later chairman of the Civil Aeronautics Board. Richard Neustadt went on to Harvard to become one of the nation's leading authorities on the presidency. You could go down the list—Phieleo Nash, who was working on minorities, was elected lieutenant governor of Wisconsin and later became commissioner of Indian Affairs. Naval aide Robert Dennison, holder of a doctor's degree in engineering, became Supreme Allied Commander in the Atlantic.

This would be a good point to define the type of individual best qualified to serve on any White House staff. First, that person ought to be a generalist in his outlook and have an ability to move easily among a wide variety of subjects. He shoud not be a special pleader nor have a particular axe to grind or keep trying to get across a pet project. I had the feeling President Carter had some people like Midge Costanza who frequently made public statements opposite from what the President believed. President Carter sort of smiled and said, "Oh, that's fine, I believe in freedom." But you have to have a little discipline if you want to have a unified program. You can't have White House staffers who are more interested in their own personal point of view, rather than the program of the President of the United States.

Of course a staff member has to be a person who loves work, not necessarily a workaholic but a person who can work after hours if necessary. His family must be understanding of the demands and priorities. But he must be mature enough not to become over-glamorized by the positon that he fills to the extent that he feels he's the source of power rather than the President of the United States. Some people working at the White House get kind of a big head, and say: "Oh, boy. I got a phrase into the President's speech, did you hear that?" This is the kind of an assistant whose usefulness to the President has ceased. A staff member has to have a deep sense of moral values, he has to have his radar out so he can anticipate where some of the booby traps and mine fields are that people are constantly creating for the White House to try to get the President in trouble.

It isn't the job of the staff member to try to read the President's mind as much as it is to help the President find out what the facts are and to clarify the opinions and the advice of the Cabinet and other officials. Also, if the President is determined, as he frequently is, to take a certain course of action the staff must have the courage to advise him about such things as the attitude of the public and of the Congress. Even though policy struggles within the staff are inevitable, a staff member has outlived his usefulness when he engages in one-upmanship to try and get closer to the throne.

Beyond that, the Brownlow-Merriam-Gulick study of the President's Committee on Administrative Management in the late 1930's has the best definition of the presidential assistant. I'm quoting from memory when they said, "A presidential assistant should have high competence, great physical vigor, and a passion for anonymity."

I wish I could give you some figures on the differing size of the White House staff. About all I can say is that it's about four times as big now as it was in Truman's time. It's difficult to make comparisons. This would be the subject of a good Ph. D. dissertation and analysis because of the changes in titles and the changes in the relationships to the President.

President Truman had a personal relation with his staff. Many Presidents try to get as far away as they can from their staff if they go away for weekends or vacations. Invariably, to the delight of junior staff memebers like myself, we had an opportunity to go to Key West, Florida and spend some relaxing days getting a piece of the President's philosophy every day and getting to question and talk with him.

Also President Truman had a knack for making the most complicated problems simple, not oversimplifying them, but getting to the heart of the matter. One day one of the presidential assistants got very agitated because he got a call from Capitol Hill at the time of the McCarthy era when a congressional committee was trying to get its hands on the raw FBI files of some personnel so that they could throw some mud around. Truman had said, no, he wasn't going to release any of that material. So this congressional committee staffer said, "Our committee is going to vote to cut off the appropriations for the White House if you don't turn over those files." In those days you could run into the President's office even though you were a junior member. The only clearance you needed was Matt Connelly telling you whether or not anybody else was in there. So this aide ran down and said, "Mr. President, I just heard some alarming news!" He related the story. President Truman was busy signing his name to some documents and he looked up and he said, "Well, you call him and tell him that we'll just use whatever money we've got and when we run out of that we'll close up." Then he went back to signing his papers as he chuckled to himself. Truman had that tremendous knack, not only for putting into down-to-earth words something that was complicated, but also in meeting problems.

I want to say a few words about the staff operation on the whistle-stop trips. These were very well-planned affairs, and Truman was always at his best with small-town crowds. In advance of the trip, themes were selected for the major, off-train speeches, and brief outlines were prepared for the shorter, rear-platform speeches. We tried to keep at least 48 hours ahead of the appearances, no more than that to keep the speeches fresh and up to date. We were well back-stopped by White House staff remaining in Washington, alerted to be able to supply the latest statistics or arguments needed as new issues came up. One of my most enjoyable tasks was to work the crowd and relay informal reactions to the President's speeches. I still can't figure out how Truman managed to give up to 15 speeches a day, spend an inordinate amount of time shooting the breeze with local politicians who boarded the train in their state or area, and somehow squeeze in enough time to sit down and chat with his staff about future stops, and catch a few catnaps along the way.

There was one aspect of Truman's staff work which I feel could have been strengthened—his relations with Congress. Perhaps because of his senatorial reaction against some of the must legislation sent up by FDR, the Supreme Court fight and the purge, when Truman became President he indicated he would prefer to handle most relations with Congress personally. In those days when Sam Rayburn ruled the House of Representatives and committee chairmen were far more powerful, it was perhaps easier to handle a great deal of these relationships personally, but it did drain a great deal of the President's time. He had congressmen coming in to talk about postmasters, what kind of pork they wanted for their districts, and other minor matters. Every week, he would have a meeting of the Big Four—Vice President Barkley, the House and Senate majority leaders and the House Speaker. Charlie Murphy the special counsel did a beautiful job preparing an agenda for these meetings, and the Capitol Hill representatives were encouraged to add anything they wanted to the agenda. In 1949, two rather ineffectual people were added to the White House staff and under Matt Connelly's direction they were made responsible for congressional liaison. I got the impression that they did more hand-holding than exerting any leadership on behalf of Truman's legislative program.

In conclusion, I want to mention one aspect of the Truman operation which is unusual when one considers that Truman was a product of the Pendergast machine and schooled in straight Democratic party politics. Murphy made an interesting statement which showed that Truman really practiced the principle that he wanted to be President of all the people and not just favor Democrats. According to Murphy:

> He just flatly refused to do anything for political reasons that he didn't think ought to be done anyway. We learned that one way to make him skittish of a proposition was to put it up to him on a political basis. He'd be suspicious right away. This was not the best way to get him to agree to anything, which I expect would surprise a good many people.

Well, I think it's about time I stopped and see if anybody has any questions or, even better, observations because a lot of you have had experience and contacts in researching and knowledge of Harry Truman that may reveal the forest rather than the trees.

QUESTION: Was there also a split on foreign policy? For instance on the Truman Doctrine, the documents indicate that on the globalization, universalization of the Truman Doctrine you seem to have had people like Clark Clifford and Senator Vandenberg outside the White House who said, "Unless we make it clear that this is a worldwide threat, the American people won't give us what we need." On the other hand you had people like George Elsey whom you mentioned, Chip Bohlen, George Kennan, and even General Marshall who said, "Well, let's define the Truman Doctrine in terms of the immediate threat and then go on from there." The documents seem to prove that. In other words, they wanted a much more discriminating formulation of the Truman Doctrine.

MR. HECHLER: I wouldn't call that a split as much as an extended discussion of alternatives. The issues were certainly discussed but not as acrimoniously as it would seem from hindsight. George Elsey also wrote a very excellent analysis of Soviet-American relations which virtually laid the basis for the developments that Truman led in 1947 and 1948: NATO and the Marshall Plan, the extension of assistance worldwide, and the setting up of SEATO in the Southeast Asia area.

I think a deeper split occurred over Point Four which was the program announced in President Truman's inaugural address in 1949 in which he enunciated the principle that the best way to fight communism was to send educational, health, and crop experts to underdeveloped nations and to spend very little money—a sort of precursor to the Peace Corps—and not to do as we're doing in El Salvador today to try and settle those problems with the force of arms. He got into a lot of arguments with Robert Lovett who was then number two man in the State Department. But I don't think there was quite as much of a deep split over the Truman Doctrine. There was discussion but not as much as a strong split at the time. Maybe my remarks are conditioned by the fact that I did not join the White House staff until 1949, two years after the Truman Doctrine was promulgated.

QUESTION: You mentioned the sheer complexities of the problems, the conflicts President Truman had to face compared to what exists today. A major factor that Acheson pointed out one time is the speed with which Britain pulled out of Greece. He said, "I had to pull that figure (300 billion for the Greek/Turkey agreement) right out of the air." He said, "We had no planning on that. The British had handled the thing and boom! they were gone, just overnight practically." I think Truman must have done a brilliant job, looking back on the staff he had at the time. It suddenly developed new dimensions that nobody had talked about.

MR. HECHLER: Yes, that's true. In addition you have to recognize that the National Security Council was not established until 1947. The Council of Economic Advisors was not established until 1947. All the work that was subsequently taken over by those bodies was done by the White House staff and of course you had a President who was a real decisionmaker. He loved to take problems and work them out and come to very quick decisions and certainly in the Truman Doctrine, that necessitated speedy action because of the precipitous British decision to pull out of the Mediterranean area.

QUESTION: As I recall you said that the President's staff was divided into the east wing and the west wing, with Steelman as the east and Clifford for the west wing. You also said, "East is east and west is west, never the twain shall meet." That suggests that there was friction. Am I wrong in that?

MR. HECHLER: There was some friction. It was the conservatives versus liberals concerning how fast the President should move. National health insurance is a good example of that and civil rights is another example. Here were two issues which really disrupted the Democratic party, and the mid-term election in 1950 which was a disaster for the Democrats as well as the election in 1946 showed that there were large sections of people in conservative areas. In the Middle West, Indiana for example, we lost a lot of congressmen in 1950 because of what was labeled "socialized medicine." How fast do you go to exercise leadership and still retain your majority? It is interesting that Truman, aside from his dislike of polls that grew out of the 1948 election, just disliked the idea of polls in general to test how people were thinking or guide his approach to issues.

There was a little memorandum that he wrote which is out at the Truman Library, stating: "I wonder how far Moses would have gone if he had taken a poll in Egypt? Where would the Reformation have gone if Martin Luther had taken a poll? It isn't polls or public opinion alone of the moment that counts. It is right and wrong, and leadership—men with fortitude, honesty and a belief in the right that make epochs in the history of the world." So there was friction which occurred over how fast to proceed on issues. Truman believed in the last analysis in raising the banner of presidential leadership.

On the eighth of May on President Truman's birthday, each year they present the Truman public service award to some individual who has best exemplified Truman's philosophy. This year it went to Martin Luther King's widow, Coretta King. She described her strong support for President Truman's civil rights policies. She best described it this way. When Strom Thurmond was asked why he was so bitterly against Harry Truman and had supported FDR, Thurmond responded, "But Truman really *means* it!"

QUESTION: Would you tell us some about how the President looked at the situation following the 1946 election where the Democrats had lost the majority in both the House and the Senate and there was a Democratic President having to face that situation. Did he develop a strategy for dealing with this? Was it basically confrontational as it was pictured later? Or how did he play between the domestic sphere and the foreign policy sphere? And then if I can further comment on the whole business, how did he then go ahead and decide what he was going to do in 1948, whether to run again?

MR. HECHLER: First of all, in November of 1946 President and Mrs. Truman received the bad news as they were coming back on the train from Independence after voting. Do you know when they got back to the Union Station in Washington, not a single member of the Cabinet was there? There were two wire service reporters, and papers blowing around in the wind. And Assistant Secretary of State Dean Acheson was the only person at the train. So Harry Truman said, "Dean, get in the car, we're going down to the White House." When they got down there the White House staff began to talk about strategy after the 1946 election defeat.

Some of the "political hawks" on the White House staff said, "What we ought to do is send up a bunch of nominations while the Democrats are still in control of Congress and get them through fast before the Republicans take over in January." Acheson advocated caution at that time and the President agreed to accept the results, but not to go as far as Senator Fulbright who suggested that he resign after appointing Vandenberg secretary of state. But then they all went down to Key West and this gave an opportunity, as Key West always did, to regroup and think through a more positive strategy. The fight with John L. Lewis occurred about the time Truman was down at Key West and that brought him up a little bit in public support.

When the Eightieth Congress convened, Truman began to see how bad things were and how the Republicans were knocking down all of the Truman domestic programs. He came down here to Charlottesville on the 4th of July in 1947 and made a speech at Monticello on Thomas Jefferson. When he got back he found that the situation was getting worse in Congress. In one of his letters he wrote to "Dear Bess" on the twelfth of July 1947, he calling Dick Russell and some of the other southerner senators gutting his domestic programs "Demopublicans" and he wrote, "You know Senator Harry Byrd had the monumental gall to insert himself beside me at Charlottesville for a picture?"

Then the "rich man's tax bill" came up, the Republican-sponsored tax bill which President Truman vetoed. He began to stake out positions supporting the average people throughout the nation—consumers, workers, farmers, small businessmen—while Congress was taking opposite positions. Along about that time a Washington lawyer named James Rowe, a partner in Tommy Corcoran's law firm, had a number of interviews with labor and other political leaders about strategy for 1948 and he wrote an excellent memorandum that's virtually the blueprint for the 1948 campaign. He sent it over to Clark Clifford. Clifford, realizing the strong, bitter feeling Truman had against Corcoran, crossed out Jin Rowe's name and added a few paragraphs at the beginning and signed his own name to the memorandum and sent it on to the President.

But regardlesss of who wrote the strategy memorandum, I think that Harry Truman had the political instincts to realize that this was the only way that he could articulate the difference between the Republican and Democratic parties and to arouse the country to such an extent as to win in 1948.

QUESTION: What about the domestic and foreign policy side? How did he play one against the other there? He had successes in the foreign policy side, wasn't he worried he might lose on the foreign policy side with a real confrontation on the domestic?

MR. HECHLER: Yes, he was concerned about it but after all there is only one President and one election and he took a gamble on that. As I indicated the Republicans were not apprehensive at all about the political consequences of supporting him on foreign policy. First of all, Vandenberg was able to get enough Republicans to support him, and to persuade some of the others to come along with the argument: "Well, he won't be President after 1948 anyway so don't worry about it." So I think the domestic confrontations with the Eightieth Congress highlighted the issues emphasized in the whistle-stop campaign that brought him victory in 1948.

Here is another "Dear Bess" letter dated July 9, 1948 just before the Democratic Convention wherein he writes: "These birds around me here have all turned politicians and precinct captains and they know nothing about it." Well, Truman had a clear idea about 1948 political strategy. He was unquestionably the best politician around there.

QUESTION: I wonder if I can jump back to Harry Vaughan. I wondered if you could explain why Truman kept him on the way he did. Was it a personal friendship?

MR. HECHLER: Yes. It was a very, very close personal friendship plus. I always marvelled at the ability of Vaughan really to raise Truman's spirits at the end of a long day by his inexhaustible collection of stories, imitations and characterizations at which Vaughan was such a expert. Although I got pretty close to Vaughan and got a belly laugh from all his stories, it is still hard for me to understand how a person like that who didn't have the class that the rest of the White House staff had could be kept on.

Truman as you know loved to play poker and Vaughan was a good guy to have around to keep the poker games full of fun. One of Vaughan's constructive accomplishments was to help bring Winston Churchill over to his alma mater (Westminster College) to give that iron curtain speech in Fulton, Missouri. That was a thing that probably couldn't have been done without Vaughan, but I don't excuse Truman for the excessive amount of loyalty that caused him to keep Vaughan.

QUESTION: Do you think that there is any merit in the proposal that the Congress should seriously reexamine and update technically the Point Four Program for Central America as an alternative to a military solution?

MR. HECHLER: I certainly do. You put your finger on a very crucial issue. I think that would be the way to go.

Changing the subject briefly, I want to add to what I said about staff recruitment.

I might mention that the Bureau of the Budget formed a wonderful recruiting ground. David Bell. David Stowe, Dick Neustadt, Harold Enarson, Milton Kayle, Russell Andrews, and myself, were all alumni of the Bureau of the Budget. In the Bureau of the Budget (which is now Office of Management and Budget) everybody had to look at problems from a broad perspective above the agency level. This proved to be very useful. Then there was Budget Director James Webb's desire to ingratiate himself with the White House by saying to the President: "You can have anybody you want on my staff," and Truman grabbed them.

QUESTION: My adult political life started with hearing Truman speak from the back of the train in 1948 and I've always been puzzled by why the acrimony against Truman. Now I recognize all the things of his decisiveness and his cutting through phony issues to get to the heart of things which would damage some people's sense of propriety. But I really can't understand the criticism. Maybe it's a resentment that we continued in the world crisis. Do you have any thoughts or are you puzzled at all the way I am by this vitriolic feeling? It still seems to be there.

MR. HECHLER: There are several things about that. First, of course his salty language insulted a lot of people and really shocked me a great deal. Very briefly, the first time I had dinner with President Truman after I'd been in the White House a short time, he said he wanted to have his speechwriters over. There were about half a dozen of us. Mrs. Truman was in Independence and he said he was lonely and didn't want to eat alone so we came over to Blair House where he was staying while they were repairing the White House. After dinner he began to play the piano. He began to play a little Chopin and I looked up at the wall and here were the portraits of Thomas Jefferson, James Madison, and James Monroe, and here was the President of the United States playing the piano just for us. He looked at me and he didn't like people to get that kind of feeling and I could tell he was going to try to bring me down to earth so he said, "You know, if I hadn't gotten in trouble by getting into politics I would have made a hell of a good piano player in a whorehouse." That's the kind of language that the average person feels is terribly undignified for the President of the United States. Well, he didn't talk like that in mixed company and he had great respect for the dignity of the presidential office, but when he was playing poker he could explode with army barracks language.

I was always struck by what seemed like an ambivalence in Truman's personality. If you watched him at a poker game or relaxing at Key West, he seemed like an old shoe, with occasional flashes of what sounded like prejudice, or comments which revealed irritation with people he had to deal with. He was the most genuinely modest person I have ever known, frequently making comments like "I never forgot where I came from or where I'm going back to," and Mrs. Truman had a great deal of influence over persuading him to come back to Independence and enjoy 19 years of post-presidential retirement living.

I often marvelled at the way in which this modest man with a grade school education rose to great heights when faced with the challenges of the presidency. My conclusions about this ambivalence in Harry Truman were best articulated by Pulitzer prize-winning author John Hersey, who wrote the following after spending several days from dawn to dusk watching President Truman operate in the fall of 1950:

> President Truman seemed to think of himself sometimes in the first person and sometimes in the third—the latter when he had in mind a personage he still seemed to regard, after nearly four years in office, as an astonishing tenant in his own body: the President of the United States. Toward himself, first-personally, he was at times mischievous and disrespectful, but he revered this other man, his tenant, as a noble, history-defined figure. Here was a separation of powers within a single psyche, and a most attractive phenomenon it was, because Harry Truman moved about in constant wonder and delight at this awesome stranger beneath his skin. And to some extent this wonder and delight must have elevated and purged the mere man.

Getting back to your question of the vitriolic feeling against Truman, of course he stepped on a lot of toes, too. That's certainly another reason. Anybody who does that—as Roosevelt found out—stirs a lot of acrimony.

QUESTION: Is it true that he said he had only three people he hated? One was somebody from Missouri that ran against him early on, and one was Richard Nixon because he called him a traitor, and the third one was Billy Graham. He was asked, "Why Billy Graham?" and he said, "Well, he goes around claiming that he's a friend of mine and he's no goddam friend of mine," or something like that. It was more colorful.

MR. HECHLER: I think he said that about Lloyd Stark who ran against him for Senate in 1940, although I didn't hear him say that personally. But I heard him say that about Nixon and he said some worse things about Nixon. He had a very strong feeling about hypocrites. He wasn't saying that Graham was a hypocrite as much as he didn't like people who wrapped religious mantles around themselves in public.

I remember once in 1952 we were coming into Parkersburg, West Virginia and all of a sudden he said he wanted to get a Bible. It seemed I was the only one on the train who had a Bible. Anyway I said, "Mr. President, is there anything I can find for you?" "No," he said, "I know where it is. St. Matthew, Chapter VI." He turned to that passage about "When thou prayest, enter into thy closet and pray to thy Father in secret." In other words, don't go out into the streets and pray loudly like the hypocrites. He used that as a text of his speech and he was really talking about John Foster Dulles at that time. He just didn't like people who beat their chest and said, "I'm more moral and more religious than you are." He added that his grandfather used to tell him that when you heard someone praying loudly in public "you had better go home and lock your smokehouse."

I'll tell you where that came from. His first job working in Clinton Brothers Drug Store when he was eleven years old was to clean the dust off the bottles up on the shelf. Occasionally leading citizens of Independence would come into the drug store and put down a dime to get a drink of liquor. They would look around furtively to see if anybody was watching. These were people who wouldn't dare to be seen in a saloon, and Truman resented this hypocrisy.

QUESTION: I remember it more precisely. He said he didn't like Billy Graham because he said, "He'd been a friend of every President since Roosevelt."

QUESTION: Do you think that his victory in 1948 could have been attributed to some extent to the split in the Republican party?

MR. HECHLER: Well, he certainly took advantage of that and tried to make sure that that split was emphasized and underlined. One of the ways he did that was by calling a special session of Congress after the conventions and reading the Republican platform which had been dictated by Dewey which promised action on aid to education, housing, civil rights, and other issues. Then President Truman in his acceptance speech said, "Well, they say they are for all these things. Now I'm going to give them an opportunity to carry them out." And of course the Congress was controlled by Taft and this really emphasized that Taft/Dewey split. But of course the split in the Democratic party was nothing to sneeze at either. We had Henry Wallace and Strom Thurmond there, too. And that made it tough but I think the Republican split really helped. But the campaign couldn't have been successfully won without the whistle-stop trip.

QUESTION: Could you talk a little bit about Truman's attitude towards Eisenhower and, more specifically, do you think Truman would have stepped aside in 1948 if Eisenhower had said something seriously about running either as a Republican or a Democrat?

MR. HECHLER: That's a very interesting question because Truman's respect for Eisenhower as a military leader was very, very high and it comes through constantly. Of course he appointed him the commander of NATO in 1951 and put full confidence in him. The reason for their split was over Senator McCarthy's attacks on General Marshall as a traitor and Eisenhower's reluctance and silence in failing to defend Marshall. This came to a head when Candidate Eisenhower put a paragraph of praise for General Marshall in one of the campaign speeches he was to deliver at Milwaukee, Wisconsin in 1952 and after it had been released to the press he took that phrase out, making it sound as though he didn't really mean it. Also, Eisenhower infuriated Truman by urging that the entire ticket in Wisconsin including the U.S. Senator Joe McCarthy be relected. This was the source of the split.

Now the second part of your question as to whether he would not have run in 1948 had Eisenhower agreed to be a candidate, certainly not if Eisenhower had run as a Republican. As a Democrat, I don't know quite how to answer that. That is what Roosevelt would have called an iffy question, I guess.

QUESTION: Do you know if Truman in fact made overtures towards Eisenhower before the 1948 election?

MR. HECHLER: I think he did, much earlier in 1945, yes. I wasn't there so I can't really document this. But there is some indication that he did tell General Eisenhower in 1945 when he went over to Potsdam and met the SHAEF Commander, General Eisenhower, that he would do anything for him that he could and that included possibly 1948. At least that's what Eisenhower recalls.

QUESTION: You mentioned a few minutes ago that in 1940 Roosevelt tried to get Truman out of the senatorship and into the Interstate Commerce Commission. Why was he given the vice presidency, then, in 1944 when according to two or three of the speakers I've heard here, Roosevelt knew and everybody knew that Roosevelt would not survive the next term?

MR. HECHLER: I don't think Roosevelt knew he would not survive, but perhaps a lot of other people did.

QUESTION: The question is this. If there was a reasonable possibility that Roosevelt would not survive the term which I think there was, very obviously, that meant that Roosevelt was making Truman President. I'm curious how that ties in to what you said he did four years earlier.

MR. HECHLER: I don't think Roosevelt thought of Truman as his successor. I really think that Roosevelt felt that weekends at Hyde Park and swimming at Warm Springs would enable him to restore his health. Truman was picked as an afterthought. Of course there is one very important thing that happened between 1940 and 1944 and that is the Truman Committee which gained a national reputation for him for saving fifteen billion dollars and conducting a really class operation as chairman of that committee. He had his picture on the cover of *Time* and was well-respected as a hard-working senator.

Also, the reason Truman was chosen by Roosevelt in 1944 was not because he would make a good successor but because he didn't have the political handicaps which other candidates like Henry Wallace, William O. Douglas, and James F. Byrnes had. Byrnes was a renegade Catholic who had strong labor opposition. Truman was the lesser evil.

QUESTION: The appointment of Jimmy Byrnes as secretary of state was one of Truman's greatest mistakes. Did he suffer from "Potomac Fever" or was it that he didn't have a very high regard for Truman?

MR. HECHLER: Well, you know Byrnes expected to get the nomination for vice president in 1944 and that creates a kind of psychological attitude toward the man who gets it that, "Here I am, I should have got what you got." That was the first problem. The second problem was that after his briefing of President Truman on such things as Yalta, Byrnes pretty well went off on his own as Secretary of State. We used to have an expression, "The State Department fiddles while Byrnes roams." He really outdid Henry Kissinger in his hopping around without keeping the President of the United States informed. What broke the camel's back was when Byrnes sent word to Charlie Ross, President Truman's press secretary, when he returned from a conference in Moscow in December 1945 saying, "Charlie, will you arrange for me to get a national radio hookup? I want to report to the people on what I accomplished.'' Imagine the secretary of state doing that before even reporting to the President. That's what really broke the relationship.

Clearly and definitely, Truman didn't want the vice presidency. He loved the Senate. He was for Jimmy Byrnes for vice president in 1944 and he consented to make the nominating speech for Byrnes at the convention. It wasn't until Roosevelt called him on the phone and twisted his arm and told him that he had to get in there, that Truman changed his mind.

QUESTION: Could you comment on the relationships between Dean Acheson and Harry Truman, two opposites?

MR. HECHLER: Oh, that's a beautiful story. Acheson was a graduate of Groton and Harvard and Yale Law School, where he had the finest education and really showed it and exuded it, whereas Harry Truman was the only President in the twentieth century who didn't get beyond high school, yet he was one of the best self-educated Presidents. There was mutual respect there. Truman was attracted to Acheson by the incident I described after the 1946 election. Politicians love this kind of personal loyalty. Acheson respected Truman's comprehension of the big picture of foreign policy and his ability as a decisionmaker. Truman respected Acheson's realization that the job of secretary of state is not to make policy like Byrnes tried to do independently. Acheson kept Truman fully briefed with facts and background, and sensed where the decisionmaking power rested.

Acheson told me the story about how he got appointed secretary of state after the 1948 election. Truman called him over to Blair House where Truman was then living and Truman said, "Dean, I want you to sit down because I have something very important I want to ask of you. I want you to be my secretary of state." Acheson then said, "Well, what about General Marshall? He's in there now." "Oh, his health is bad, he just had a kidney removed." "Well, what about Averell Harriman? What about Fred Vinson? What about Lewis Douglas or William O. Douglas?" He went down a list of people, suggesting: "One of those people would be better." Finally, Truman said, "Look, there are ten thousand people in this country that are better able to be President of the United States than I am but I happen to President and I want you to be my secretary of state and that's the end of it."

MR. THOMPSON: We want to thank Ken Hechler who has been a moving spirit and leader in the political science profession ever since I can remember. He was willing and able to talk to people who were leaders in the profession but also those who had their careers ahead of them. Obviously his work in the Congress and in the executive branch and now his important book on Truman all form contributions which will live in the future as we think about this presidency and about the government of the United States.

THE TRUMAN BUDGET
Elmer Staats

MR. THOMPSON: We are very pleased to welcome you to a forum with Elmer Staats on President Harry S. Truman and the Truman approach to the budget. When we took a poll of Truman presidency watchers among those who have kept themselves informed about the *dramatis personae* of the Truman administration, one name kept appearing whenever we asked whom we should have speak to us about the Truman presidency. Elmer Staats was mentioned as a person who had seen both the political and the public administration side as well as the fiscal and the budgetary side of the Truman administration as no one else in government had done. And so we tried early on to invite Elmer Staats to speak to us on this subject. I'd like to ask Frederick Mosher to introduce Mr. Staats. Fritz Mosher has just finished a very important book for the Miller Center entitled *A Tale of Two Agencies* which compares the GAO and the OMB. He also is heading up a task force on what we hope will be the third of our national commissions, this one on presidential transitions and their impact on the formulation of foreign policy. So not only does he know Mr. Staats as well or better than anyone in the room but he also is very much a part of our Miller Center group—Mr. Mosher.

MR. MOSHER: Thank you, Ken. In spite of the fact that Elmer Staats has been invited to talk about the Truman administration I think it should be understood that he is not confined in his knowledge and experience to the Truman administration. The fact of the matter is he worked for five Presidents starting with Roosevelt. He was deputy director of the budget under four different Presidents including Truman, Eisenhower, Kennedy, and Johnson and then he was a comptroller general of the United States. He had the top position in the GAO for fiteen years during four more presidencies starting again with Johnson, Nixon, Ford, Carter, and Reagan. He retired two years ago (1981) and he is now the chairman or a member of three or four dozen boards.

He has an absolutely unique reputation in Washington. He is a political career public servant from way, way back. When he was appointed by President Johnson to be comptroller general, the Budget Bureau threw a party for him honoring his departure and their gift to him was a seat cushion one side of which was an elephant and on the other side was a donkey. So I think he will probably not give us a partisan talk. It is a great pleasure to introduce Mr. Elmer Staats.

MR. STAATS: Thank you, Fritz. I think this is a particularly appropriate time to be reviewing the record and the history of the Truman period. On May 8, 1984 we will be celebrating the Truman centennial. Plans are already going forward with respect to ways to observe that centennial. I'm serving on the executive committee of the Truman centennial committee chaired by Clark Clifford who served as special counsel for President Truman. It will be of interest to you to know that we still have four living ex-Cabinet members who served in the Truman administration, all of them serving on this committee. We have a hundred and thirty-three individuals who are serving on the overall committee.

The focus on our discussion today is on Truman's interest and role in the federal budget. I find it difficult to separate the discussion about the Truman period from some of the events that took place prior to his presidency, particularly during the period of the Roosevelt administration. As implied by what Fritz has said, the Bureau of the Budget and the General Accounting Office were twin agencies established by legislation enacted in 1921 called the Budget and Accounting Act. This act essentially was an idea of Woodrow Wilson's, growing, perhaps more than anything else, out of the growth of government during World War I but also out of his background as a political science professor at Princeton and governor of New Jersey. But be that as it may, the Bureau of the Budget was set up to serve the President and the General Accounting Office was set up to serve the Congress. The Bureau of the Budget was located in the Treasury Department. I suppose this was logical because Treasury was the source of revenue but also there was no place else to put it. The Brownlow Commission which was appointed by Roosevelt to look at the structure of government recommended that there be established an Executive Office of the President to assist the President and the theme of that report was "The President needs help." So grouped into the Executive Office—in addition to the White House Office—were the Bureau of the Budget which was pulled out of the Treasury Department, the National Resources Planning Board which is concerned with economic and resource planning (it was chaired by an uncle of FDR, Fredrik Delano) an Office of Government Reports which was set up to report progress on recovery from the [recession and] depression, and a Liaison Office for Personnel Management. This constituted the Executive Office of the President plus six administrative assistants in the White House proper who were pledged to be anonymous, to have "a passion for anonymity," a phrase that became famous for that reason.

The Bureau of the Budget at that time was an agency that simply pulled together all of the requests that emerged from the agencies. It had a very little staff, a total staff of thirty-five people and that included nonprofessional as well as professional so you could easily see it could not be an effective agency. In the Executive Office the charter for the Bureau of the Budget was outlined in an executive order which the President approved. As a footnote, the Executive Office probably could not have been brought about except with the great persuasiveness of Senator Byrnes, who later became Chief Justice and one of the key supporters of the President, because there was a lot of opposition to this. People were concerned it was going to create an instrumentality for the President to, in effect, be a dictator.

I served under four budget directors during the Truman period. Harold Smith was brought in by Roosevelt on the recommendations of the Brownlow Committee. He did not know Smith at all. Smith was a Republican but Roosevelt didn't seem to be bothered with this. He said, "I want the best budget director to be found anywhere in the country." Smith served during the period up to June 1946 when he left the executive branch to go to be Executive Vice President of the World Bank. He was succeeded by Jim Webb who was brought in from the Treasury Department, had been in private industry and served on the Hill. He was a friend of John Snyder's who was secretary of the treasury at that time. Webb served from 1946 to late 1948 when he became under secretary of state. Frank Pace succeeded Jim Webb. He was there first as a deputy director and then later as director. He went over to be secretary of the Army. Truman then appointed a career person out of the bureau, Frederick Lawton, to be director and myself as a deputy director. This was in March of 1950 and we served in that capacity through the rest of the Truman period.

That gives you a bit of a background. I did not know President Truman before he became President. I observed him as chairman of the Truman Investigating Committee on the Hill. Few of us had any idea that he would become vice president. My first indication of this was brought about in a rather strange way. One of my functions in the bureau as a career person was concerned with the civilian war agencies in the government including the Office of War Mobilization which was headed up by Justice Byrnes. I had an appointment to go see him one afternoon and had made an appointment through his administrative assistant, a woman named Cassie Connor. I arrived and she said, "He'll be right with you" and pretty soon she went into the office and came back and said, "Well I think it is still alright but it's going to be a little while, I think." Eventually she came back out and said, "I think we better make this appointment for another time." And it turned out that Eleanor Roosevelt was in there trying to calm him down when he was told that he was not going to be on the slate. Truman was going to be the vice president.

As I mentioned, Harold Smith was a distinguished budget director. He had very close relationship with President Roosevelt and he had a concept of the budget that placed emphasis on the management role of the bureau as well as the budget role of the bureau. During the war period the Bureau of the Budget was about the only staff resource the President had up until 1953 when the Office of War Mobilization was established. So the bureau grew very rapidly during this period. From this forty-five number that I mentioned, by the end of the war he had something over six hundred people in the bureau. Smith retired, largely for financial reasons. You have to keep in perspective that at the time the budget director got $10,000 and he had a growing family. The World Bank would pay him a lot more. He had a farm down here near Charlottesville and he decided he had worked hard enough and left. My point is that there was no difference of policy between him and President Truman.

Webb came in with no preconception about the bureau. He had some things he wanted to do but he was wise enough to realize that he had better take his time and after a short time he began to get his sense of direction. One of the things he wanted to do was to bring the Budget Bureau more closely in touch with the staff of the White House and that was a very significant change. He did this of course with Truman's full blessing and full support. So there emerged from this philosophy an increasing number of staff contacts with the White House staff. Smith never took anyone except his deputy to see the President and the staff saw the President—if at all—only on a social occasion. Staff contacts between the White House and the Bureau of the Budget were minimal but this changed with Webb. He started taking staff members with him when he had appointments with the President at intermediate and senior levels of the staff. Truman liked this and he was relaxed with it and it seemed to fit his own style or method of operating. The bureau then began to detail staff to the White House and there was a relatively large number of Budget Bureau staff who went over to serve on the White House staff; David Stowe, Dick Neustadt, David Bell, Harold Henderson, Ken Hechler who later became a congressman and so on. All of these people were career people in the bureau and went over to work in different capacities in the White House.

Now this had some pluses and minuses with it. Because as these people moved out of the Budget Bureau over to the White House staff, they didn't have staff, they were inclined to call up their friends back in the bureau to do various chores for them. They wouldn't always necessarily bother to talk to the director or the deputy director about these requests so there was some slight strain and tension there but overall the benefits of this free style paid off very well.

It was during this period also that we conceived the idea of having a legislative program of the President in addition to the budget program. There had been a legislative reference office in the Bureau but it never had been in a positive role. It reviewed various bills that came up for presidential signature summarizing the pros and cons and the departmental positions on those bills but it was not a positive role in the sense that it had any outreach functions. Some of us felt that if we are going to have a budget program for the President there ought to be also, along with, it a legislative program. For one thing legislation cost money. And the other question was to be sure that the executive branch is speaking with one voice before the Congress, instead of having each agency go off sometimes in conflicting positions. So we developed a legislative program. I became the head of the Legislative Reference Office in 1947 and brought in Roger Jones as my deputy and Dick Neustadt as an assistant and it was our job to try to develop this program.

We did this in part as an institutional product, getting the views of all the elements of the Bureau of the Budget, but we sent out a call for proposals from all of the agencies. Anything that was going to cost an estimated ten million dollars we asked them to put on that list. And we would show those items that the President was going to support right in the budget as a part of the budget total. That concept is still in existence today. We worked in this capacity very closely with Clark Clifford who was, as I mentioned, counsel to the President, and his assistant at that time was Charles Murphy who later succeeded him. The bureau became in a sense an adjunct to the White House staff and in fact one time we debated seriously whether this legislative coordination program function ought not to be actually moved over to the White House. Murphy and I agreed that that probably was not wise because we would lose a very valuable ingredient, namely the input which the professional staff of the bureau could contribute. At least we'd run the risk of doing that and besides if the change of administration came along the chances of that surviving in the White House would not be very great and you would lose the continuity which could be very important.

So the bureau became increasingly involved in presidential messages, drafting of proposed legislation, working in close tandem with the White House staff. That was an important development.

Another important development was the change in the internal structure of the Bureau of the Budget during this period. In 1952 we decided that the bureau should be organized more along programmatic lines. So we developed a number of divisions, one on national defense another one on health and human resources, education, and so forth; divisions of this type where we could bring together the professional staff concerned with different program areas of the federal government. And that came to be what might be called "line divisions." We had an Office of Budget Review which became the budget preparation unit which coordinated with each of these divisions, the legislative reference division which I mentioned, a division of statistical standards which was concerned with coordination of the collection of data by the government from all sources in the country. We developed during this period an advisory commission on management improvement. These were people from the private sector, business people for the most part. But the main significance of this reorganization was to establish some of these line divisions.

Let me move to try to place the Bureau of the Budget in the framework of changes in the Executive Office of the President that took place during this period of time. Toward the end of the war, as many of you will recall, there was great concern about the ability of the economy to change from a wartime footing to a peacetime footing. There were estimates of high unemployment ranging up to eighteen million people unemployed. So the Congress became restive and Senator O'Mahoney in particular had hearings which led to the establishment of the Council of Economic Advisers in the Employment Act of 1946. Harold Smith was opposed to this because he could not see how you could develop the budget out of the context of the economy as a whole. He did not look favorably upon this at all. Some of us did not agree with that position but nevertheless Congress established a three member Council of Economic Advisers which was supposed to be bipartisan in nature and which was to analyze the economy of what needed to be done to make for conditions of higher employment. That was 1946.

The National Security Act in 1947 and 1949 created two new bodies in the Executive Office. One was the National Security Council and the other was the National Security Resources Board, the latter attempting to be, as the name implies, a board which was going to concern itself with the ability of the economy to mobilize, have adequate resources such as stockpiles and things of this nature.

There was also during this period in the early fifties concern about whether the government was focusing adequately on the field of science and President Truman asked us to study the matter and give him a recommendation. It was from that study that the science adviser was established in 1950 and through various transformations that office is still in existence today. The Office of Defense Mobilization was created in 1950 growing out of the Korean hostilities period. It later became the Office of Civil and Defense Mobilization and assumed the civil defense function later on during the Eisenhower period. These important developments took place during the Truman administration.

A telecommunications advisor was set up in 1951 which then was later moved to the Office of Defense Mobilization by President Eisenhower. The Office of War Mobilization Reconversion, which I mentioned was headed up initially by Justice Byrnes, later toward the end of the war became concerned more with the conversion of the economy. John Steelman became the head of this and his job was essentially to try to map out a strategy for converting wartime programs to peacetime programs. Since I was concerned with the organization of the war agencies I was given the job of trying to demobilize the Office of War Mobilization. We developed an executive order to try to merge the residue of this office with the White House staff. The reason I mention this is I think of some interest. We worded the executive order to outline John Steelman's functions as "Assistant to the President." When I sat down with him to review the wording of it the first thing that caught his eye was "Assistant to the President." He wrote in the word "The" in front of it. This came up later because that title "The" was kept on and given to Sherman Adams in the Eisenhower administration but there was some little tension at the time about whether Steelman was *the* assistant to the President, particularly in the light of Clark Clifford's role as "Special Counsel to the President."

I will mention two other organizational developments during this period which I think are significant because they all impinge on President Truman's responsibilities for the budget. It was about 1950 that he asked Averell Harriman to come back to Washington to be an adviser in the National Security area. Later the Congress ratified this function and created the position of "Director for Mutual Security," which was to coordinate our economic and military assistance programs to other countries. Harriman was an important addition to this staff and we worked with him closely on the military and foreign aid budgets. He played a very prominant role in that period of time.

One other development. It was in 1949 that the CIA functions were defined to report to the National Security Council. The charter for the CIA embraced both covert operations as well as intelligence operations. The Joint Chiefs of Staff were not happy about this and they felt that there should be separate agencies concerned with intelligence and covert operations. They developed a proposal they sent to President Truman to set up such separate offices so that they would be in effect on a coequal basis. The State Department was not happy about this proposal and obviously the CIA was not happy about it. President Truman set up a task force with Admiral Sidney Souers as his liaison with the intelligence community; General Beedle Smith, then the Director of CIA; Allen Dulles, his deputy; and myself, to see what we thought of this idea—whether any part of it or all of it should be adopted. Our proposal was to set up a Psychological Strategy Board which would be a coordinating board of all of the informational, covert, and defense functions involving foreign affairs. Gordon Gray who was then secretary of the Army was made the head of this. The Psychological Strategy Board then became in the Eisenhower administration the Operations Coordinating Board for which I was the staff director.

I mentioned these because in the Executive Office we had emerging a number of different entities and personalities that had to be somehow worked into the budget process. This of course fell heavily upon a budget director to make certain that what was emerging in the form of a budget recommendation was in consonance with the views of other elements of the Executive Office. This was not an easy thing to do. It worked out on the whole quite well. Webb set the basic framework for this which Frank Pace and Frederick Lawton who succeeded him continued. It was a rather rapidly moving area and one which I think tends to emphasize a point that the Executive Office has to serve the incumbent President and he has to have freedom to bring in individuals or create mechanisms or organizations that will support his policy objectives.

I would like to say a special word about the Council of Economic Advisers because its work in particular impinged upon the economic assumptions that went into the federal budget. The first chairman was Edwin Nourse who was brought from the Brookings Institution. He was a Republican. Leon Keyperling was a Democratic member and Clark was a Democrat, he was a businessman, an oil man from Wyoming. Norris' concept was that Council of Economic Advisers had to be completely objective, be a non-advocate and neutral politically. Keyperling didn't agree with that at all. He was a hundred and eighty degrees different in his perspective overall. This created a lot of tension which spilled over on us in the Budget Bureau because we never knew quite who was calling the shots. Keyperling, being an activist, would be more likely to take the initiative in coming to see us.

Robert Turner, who had been on Steelman's staff, had moved over with Steelman to the White House. He was from the University of Indiana and had been associated closely with the War Production Board and later became assistant director of the budget in the Kennedy period. It fell to him to try to mediate among these three members of the Council. His role was not a happy one because it fell to him to edit the two reports which were provided for under the Employment Act. One part was a presidential report which was to be what the President thought and recommended. The other was the council's report which was supposed to be analytical and objective and factual in nature. But there had to be some way to be sure they weren't saying different things. So Bob Turner's job was to try to edit the council's report here and that created problems. The Budget Bureau arrangement with the council was eased a great deal when two of its senior economists were transferred to the council staff—we did this deliberately to try to make the relationship easier—Arthur Smithies who later taught at Harvard and Gerhard Colm, both of them were able economists.

Later Nourse decided he had had enough and resigned. Keyperling then replaced him. That changed things. In areas like housing, for example, that Keyperling had a particular interest in, he was on our doorstep all the time trying to either get legislation proposed or more money in the budget.

Related to this and part of the reason I bring it up is to ask now encompassing should the Bureau of the Budget be and how broad should the OMB role be? If you look at budgeting as a whole it represents the totality of the President's policy and program. Obviously the President needs input from different perspectives and the view that I had and I think that was shared by Webb and Pace and Lawton was that the bureau should not try to encompass everything. So we were on the side generally of encouraging, if we felt that there was a need, the organization of special staff to deal with particular areas of presidential interests: a science adviser which I mentioned, and the Council of Economic Advisers, a Telecommunication Adviser, then later in the procurement area and in the regulatory policy. Today the regulatory and procurement areas are particularly active, growing out in part of this earlier period of time but also because of specific legislation which mandated a role for the OMB.

The Treasury/budget role is always an important area but also a somewhat troublesome area. The people in the Treasury never quite forgave the fact that the Budget Bureau was no longer a part of the Treasury. The revenue function, the tax policy function, resided in the Treasury so that there was a certain amount of tension always in terms of the Treasury/budget relationship. The Webb-Snyder relationship helped a great deal in that particular period. We had to be sure that we were leaning over backwards to avoid any impression in the Treasury that we were going ahead without regard for their views. We relied on the Treasury not only to develop the estimates of revenues but their views on expenditures as well. Revenues, like expenditures, also depend a great deal on what assumptions are made about the economy, what's going to happen to interest rates and things of this type. So we had beginning in this period what was later called the "triad." We had designated individuals from the Council of Economic Advisers, the Treasury, and the Budget Bureau to work together to reach agreement on these assumptions that we would feed into the tax side as well as the expenditure side of the budget. Later the Federal Reserve Board was added to this, what was called the "quadriad" development. John Snyder was always present at the President's press conferences on the budget.

I've referred already to the importance that Harold Smith and James Webb placed on the organization and management role of the Bureau of the Budget. That was a part of the charter set forth in the Budget and Accounting Act. The question is really how to implement it? How does the bureau take the leadership in this area? Under Harold Smith the Division of Administrative Management was created with responsibility for both interagency coordination, organization, and management issues as well as the assistance to the agencies in their internal management problems—a kind of consulting type relationship.

In the 1952 reorganization, the focus became more heavily on interagency, government-wide issues with the program divisions concerned more with internal management, that is, the management consulting function.

A basic problem then and today is that the budget function crowds out the management and organization emphasis in the budget process. This is an unresolved problem, but one which needs attention. The National Academy of Public Administration put out a report at the time of the change of administration urging strongly that the management and organization role of the OMB be revitalized. To date that has not been done even though the name of the agency has changed from the Bureau of the Budget to the Office of Management and Budget. There is less management concern today in the OMB than there was back in the forties. What is the answer? One possible answer would be a "Deputy for Management" of the same status as a "Deputy for Budget." More and more people are saying they've got to pull the management function out of the OMB and create a separate unit in the Executive Office to be concerned with ways to make the government more efficient and economical.

A word about the Bureau of the Budget in terms of its political role. Harold Smith used to tell us when we were young staff people that "you have to be politically aware but not politically active." He also said the corollary to that is the best politics for any President is a nonpolitical budget bureau. What he was really saying is that the President needs a staff that has credibility outside the government and particularly in the Congress in relationship to the budget. Webb had another corollary for this and he would say, "Put yourself in the same position and the same shoes that you think the President has to put himself in when you prepare a memorandum for me to send to him asking him to approve certain recommendations." Which is to say, try to look at all the considerations that go into that decision and be aware of the kind of problems the President has to consider.

This non-political emphasis played a role because the budget director himself was not even confirmed by the Senate then. It's only in more recent years as budget directors become more political that the Congress has insisted on confirmation. Harold Smith felt so strongly about this. I'm sure he would have resigned if anybody had really pushed this idea very hard. But there was a payoff from this I thought. For example when Eisenhower became President he told the new budget director Joe Dodge that he would have complete freedom to make whatever changes he wanted to make in the Budget Bureau staff. Partly because he was there early enough to get an understanding of the bureau's role and the caliber of its staff, he was able to say, when Eisenhower asked him in January what changes he wanted to make, that he didn't want to make any changes. He was satisfied that the career staff for the bureau could serve the new administration well.

Truman had a special interest in the budget. He was on the Senate Appropriations Committee and that undoubtedly affected his interest in the budget. But he was also interested in following the budget as it was placed in operation. We developed a series of chart books, for example, a little booklet we called "The Budget in Operation." He kept it in his left-hand drawer and whenever we would come over to talk about some subject he would pull this out and if we were talking about veteran's payments or defense buildup or whatever it was, he had charts and data before him. He had a lot of interest in this. As I mentioned he held his own press conferences on the budget which I believe was unique among all the Presidents. We would give him a briefing book and meet with him the day before and then with the secretary of treasury sitting on one side, budget director on the other side, he answered the questions. It would be very rare that he would have to turn to either of them for answers.

This certainly impressed the media people, I think it had an impact because they knew it wasn't somebody else's budget, it was his budget. Something that impressed us also was his willingness to talk freely at sessions on the budget at which third and fourth level staff of the udget Bureau were present. He was not reserved and this I think was a tremendous help to the staff and the bureau because they could sense not only what the decisions were but also the kind of thinking that went into the decisions.

In terms of the overall result, we had during the Truman period there four deficit years but four surplus years also with the total adding up to about ten billion dollars in surplus for the eight year period.

One of the controversial areas in this period was the defense budget. Truman felt strongly that we ought to try to do something to reduce the federal debt which had been built up during World War II. He also felt that in the national security area that the priority should go to foreign aid, e.g., the Marshall Plan, Greece, Turkey and so forth and less to an effort to build up and maintain high levels of military forces. He related the size of our standing forces to what we had going into World War II. So his decision was to start bringing the defense establishment down. He set a ceiling on the Defense Department in 1950 of 14.4 billion dollars. I remember these figures well because we got a lot of flack about them from the Congress. And he had planned a 13.5 billion figure for 1951. I remember one day being over there and he said, "We're going to bring this down to 11 billion dollars in 1952." Well then Korea came along. How much of the Korean problem was created, as some people would argue, by the fact that our defense forces were cut back as against what had been stated to be our military and defense interests in the Far East, others will have to say. I don't really know. But the significant point here, and this created a lot of tension, was that the people in the Defense Department put together a document which came to be know as NCS 68—National Security docket number 68—which had argued for a much higher buildup in the defense forces and this became a controversy because many people felt that we had cut our forces back too far and maybe that had some part to play in causing the Korean invasion.

In general Truman did not use the collegial body of the National Security Council to work with him on budget decisions but there was one that I recall where there was an exception. The question was what kind of level of support for the foreign aid program should he support for the budget that he was preparing that was going to be turned over to the Eisenhower administration? He was somewhat concerned about this because there had been statements made in the campaign that the new administration would cut back on foreign aid. The Budget Bureau put together a document outlining the pros and cons of different levels of the foreign aid program. Instead of making that decision on his own he had a meeting in his office in the Cabinet room with Averell Harriman, Bob Lovett, the secretary of defense, the Joint Chiefs, the three service secretaries, White House staff and the Budget Bureau staff in which he let everyone around the table give their views. He decided the level before he left the room, that is what he was going to support and he went for a much higher level than some of us thought he would.

Just a few general remarks by way of summarizing my own impressions of this period and President Truman's role in the budget. One thing that impressed all of us was his great respect for the Office of the President. He would say what is important is not how this is going to affect me but how is it going to affect the office because if it affects the office then it is going to affect my successors as well. So his concern was a jealous concern about the power, the prerogatives, and the role of the presidency. This colored his views on the dangers of the legislative veto, for example. He said it was unconstitutional and he took a very strong position that the legislative veto was not constitutional. But he also argued that if the Congress appropriated more money than his budget request, he ought to have the right to withhold some of that money. In more recent years we called it impoundment. The issue that came up was a seventy-group Air Force where the Air Force was pushing hard for seventy groups. I've forgotten what the budget provided for. It wasn't nearly that high, something like 45. He was not going to let them spend it. We and the attorney general both said, "We don't think you've got authority to hold this up." He thought a little while and said, "Well, I'm Commander in Chief, am I not?" And that was it. He made his decision stick.

He had a detailed knowledge of the history of the presidency. He read a great deal of history and this always, I think, affected his thinking when these kinds of issues came up. He would frequently say to us when we had a question or decision, "Well, what's the right thing to do?" This became kind of a password for our staff: "What's the right thing to do?"

His nonpartisanship impressed us by appointments of Republicans to key positions in foreign affairs and the military and his support for career appointments. Some of you may recall that Senator McKeller and Senator Bridges led a fight in the Senate against David Lillienthal as chairman of the TVA and later against Gordon Clapp when Lillienthal retired from the position. Truman supported both of them in the strongest terms and particularly Gordon Clapp who was a career person. Bipartisanship here paid off for him because on the day that the crucial vote was to be taken it was Senator Vandenberg, a Republican, who got up on the floor and made the speech that decided the issue. Truman had a very good relationship with Vandenberg. And part of this was due to the fact that he had appointed to key positions in the Defense and State Departments individuals on a bipartisan basis.

Truman had a quick mind. Some people thought he made decisions too quickly but he was decisive and when you think back today—and I think this will come out in the centennial program—if you look at our foreign policy today and the structure in which our foreign policy is based, most all of it goes back to the Truman period. You think about the United Nations, you think about our policy in Greece and Turkey, NATO, setting up the Defense Departement, etc. All of these go back to the Truman period and basically have not been changed in the interval since.

His memory for details as I mentioned and his ability to recall from year to year without briefing what he had put in the budget the year before obviously impressed all of us. His ability to relax—he would take the budget and the final budget message with him when he went down at Christmas time to Key West. He loved to play poker and he was away from everything and he knew how to relax. I asked him one day when I was in his office, "Of all the problems that you have before you, how can you sleep at night?" And he said, "Look at that door over there. When I walk out of that door at night I leave these problems right here until I come back the next day." So he knew how to relax.

I think most of all we recall that he was a warm human being. He was non-formal in his approach. He would welcome into his office people below the director level just as easily as he would the director. And he called us "Mr. Budget." That was the kind of easy relationship that we remembered and of course admired.

MR. THOMPSON: We can't take credit because we had planned this since last summer but it is fortuitous that our discussions of the Truman presidency coincide with the very important set of activities you're launching as part of the Truman centennial. Who would like to ask the first question?

QUESTION: Mr. Staats, I've been listening to tapes of interviews with White House aides in connection with some work I'm doing on Carter and Congress and the thing that impresses me is that one question the interviewer asks of all these people is to describe their style of operation within the White House, what they expected to do, how they came into the White House. Almost to a person, they speak as though this is going to be a very short run experience for them. They expect to work extremely hard, almost burn themselves out, most of them young people and when you were describing in the early stages of the Truman administration the relationship of the Bureau of the Budget and the development of the White House staff, some people coming over from there, all I can think of is well, this sounds like a group of people much more government career-oriented to begin with, people who have a longer view of things and generally more professional. Now, is that correct or were there also sort of "burnouts" in the early Truman administration, too? Were there people who came in expecting to work sixteen to eighteen hours a day and never do that kind of work again?

MR. STAATS: Well, we worked sixteen and eighteen hours a day! It is not an easy job, particularly during the three or four months where you are intensely working on the budget. It is literally a seven day a week job. I would not accept the argument that is more intensive today than it was then because I don't think it's really a change. I do think that there has been a change in the philosophy of career vs. noncareer. One view is that the career people can serve a new administration as well because they've got the background and the continuity and detail knowledge of these programs. The other view is that you can't trust those people because they are so engrained in a particular position somewhere along the line or they've got a political connection with the previous administration that would come back to hurt them. Now instead of having a nonpolitical director and deputy director which we obtained in the Truman period, you have a political director and political deputy and associate directors, all confirmed by the Senate, and they are all regarded as political appointees. The program division directors that I describe who are the career people are now down about four levels in the hierarchy in the OMB. Now what does that mean? It means that the people who are really digging into the programs of the agencies don't have direct access to the director. That was something that we insisted on. And we would take those people with us when we went to see the President on budget decisions. We would have them directly before us in what we call the director's review where we made the markups on recommendations to the President. We felt it was essential to have that kind of firsthand relationship between the career people who worked year in and year out with the program for the agencies. I happen to feel that the results are better under the former philosophy than under the second. All of my experience would support Harold Smith's thesis that the best politics for the President is a non-political budget director and budget bureau. The OMB has lost a lot of very good people because the people became discouraged. Too many layers and too much of it being done on a straight political basis.

QUESTION: Could I pursue the points you were just making? Has there been a change over time in the professionals in terms of their capacity to serve in a non-partisan objective way? I don't think you have to limit that to the Bureau of the Budget. I'd be interested in your observations on the career civil service and the government tempo.

MR. STAATS: Well, it is dangerous for me to try to be judging the caliber, objectivity, and so forth of individuals unless I'm in an organization and so I have to beg off to some degree. But I will give you my impressions. I give you my impressions based on what a lot of people who have direct knowledge have said and that is that we have lost a terrific number of able people because they just did not feel they were getting the support that they needed from topside. I think the Stockman interview in the *Atlantic Monthly* damaged the OMB greatly. Maybe that can be overcome in time but if you look now at the places in the government where you might say the brightest and best graduates are looking to go to work, it used to be they all wanted to go to work in the Bureau of the Budget. That is not so much true today. They are getting some able young people that I know about but I don't think nearly to the extent that they did before.

QUESTION: You've touched on the National Security Council and since that time, of course it's many years now, it has become so institutionalized and in many respects it's become a policymaking body rather than advisory and in many ways under Mr. Brzezinski in President Carter's administration it preempted the State Department. Would you make any recommendations on how it might be restructured?

MR. STAATS: This issue has an interesting history. The idea of a National Security Council was not Truman's idea. In fact he rarely met with them. The statute prescribed the membership. That was another thing that irritated him. He didn't like to be dictated to as to who came to meetings in his office.

Even so, after the Korean outbreak he did meet with them. But in 1949 the membership was made more flexible so he could designate individuals. Congress took off the service secretaries, for example, and I think that eased the situation for him. In the security council you have an executive secretary. That was provided for in the statute. And when Sidney Sours was President Truman's assistant there was a career person, James Lay, who stayed on during the Eisenhower period. That was a career post.

The idea of a security council, many people suspected, was designed to try to lock the President in on positions. The council would become the decisionmaking body rather than the President. It was widely viewed that Ferdinand Eberstadt and others who has served in the war didn't trust Truman. He had been chairman of the War Investigating Committee and he wasn't another Roosevelt. There was a lot of feeling that existed at the time that the National Security Council was designed more as a mechanism to fence the President in than to give the President help. And I think Truman was quite aware of those kinds of speculations.

Over time I think the Security Council has developed into an important instrumentality. I thought it worked very well during the Eisenhower administration. As I mentioned for five years I was a part of that machinery. I sat in on the meetings of the Security Council. It's not a decisionmaking body. It can't be. The President has got to make the decisions. But it can bring to the President good staff work.

The problem in recent years, as I sense it, is that President's adviser on national security has tended to come into competition with the secretary of state. I personally think the President needs an adviser who can look at the totality of our foreign relations which includes defense and such domestic programs as agriculture, health, and a multiplicity of the aspects of U.S. domestic programs that effect foreign policy. But he ought to be working quietly in a coordinating role and a communicating role. It takes an unusual type of person not to step over that line but there is a line there that can be observed if a person and the President wants to see that line observed. Working quietly behind the scenes, not holding press conferences, and not having a big staff as Kissinger has had, Brzezinski had, and Clark has today. It is an important function but it is one where it can damage the President's ability to utilize the secretary of state and the secretary of defense effectively.

QUESTION: If an adviser hires a press secretary is that a sign he's crossed the line?

MR. STAATS: I think so. He shouldn't be out making speeches.

QUESTION: The question I had was that in most of the many roles you've played but particularly as comptroller general and in view of the budget do you see an erosion of the ability of the presidency to govern with the increased development in congressional staffs, committee staffs, and proliferation of what I've always considered the non-elected representatives and senators to Congress?

MR. STAATS: That's a good question. I think the short answer has to be yes. It stems from a number of different things. A part of it is the fact that the Congress itself is a different body than it used to be. It is over-democratized, you might say, when the caucus has to select all the subcommittee chairmen. They've lost the ability to have discipline within the parties in the Congress. Baker can't really control what goes on in the Republican side of the Senate. O'Neill can't do it in the House. The proliferation of subcommittees is a part of it and along with that the proliferation of congressional staff, a staff which has free rein to ramble all over the whole government. You never know whether you are talking about the views of a member or some person on the staff.

That's part of it and then part of it is the emergence of a philosophy that Congress needs to approve a lot of actions, either through the legislative veto or coming into agreement provisions, or in the case of money, reprogramming decisions. These all come to the Congress for approval by somebody and that somebody is not the Congress as a whole. "Somebody" is usually a subcommittee or a full committee or one house. That has eroded the President's position I think a great deal.

Take the congressional authorization process, for example. I remember being at an Eisenhower Cabinet meeting in 1954 where the decision was whether he would veto a bill which required authorization of the major program decisions in the Defense Department. Previous to that the only congressional authorizations were Corps of Engineer projects and Bureau of Reclamation projects, traditionally "back home" and highly constituency oriented. But now everything in the Defense Department, Science Foundation, and the U.S. Information Agency, are authorized annually. There is hardly a single program of the federal government that doesn't go through a double process of being authorized by the authorizing committee and funded through the appropriations committee. Those authorizations sometimes go into great detail. They almost reach the point of saying who is to be appointed and how the agencies are to be organized and administered. This intrusion by the committees into the executive branch probably is even more important in some ways than the other two considerations.

The President still has the great advantage of television. That helps him immensely.

QUESTION: How much lead time did you have from point zero until the budget was presented to the Congress?

MR. STAATS: Well, normally the budget that goes to Congress in January is for the fiscal year which starts October 1, so you are talking about twenty-two months lead time from the beginning to the end of the budget period. Before we changed the fiscal year it was eighteen months. But before that you have to do an awful lot of work leading up to the decision as to what goes into the budget.

It was during the Truman period that we began the idea of what we called a budget preview. This meant that in the spring, after the budget had gone forward to Congress, we would try to map out priorities for the budget as it would go forward to Congress in January of the following year. This preview would start in March and April. That included an effort to try to agree on economic assumptions and what major legislative programs the President might want to put into the budget. In the process we would call in the agency heads along about June with a memorandum and put these questions before them and ask them to go back and give us a memorandum on what they thought about it. The formal submission budgets were supposed to come in not later than September 15. Sometimes they did not come in that soon. That complicated our life. But that was roughly the cycle and that cycle still maintains today. That hasn't really changed. It's almost a year-round process now.

NARRATOR: Maybe we can thank Mr. Staats best by a personal reference. I once served on a committee that was going to make a public service award and naturally Mr. Staats' name was mentioned very early and then someone said, "Well, maybe we should give it to him but the only trouble is he has had every other public service award there is." This afternoon we've seen some of the reasons why. Thank you so much for your clear and insightful presentation.

III
TRUMAN'S
FOREIGN
POLICY

THE GREAT FOREIGN POLICY DECISIONS
Robert Donovan

After presiding over the Senate on April 12, 1945, Vice President Harry S. Truman was suddenly summoned to the White House without explanation. The Second World War was in its closing phase. In Europe, the Red Army was fighting on the approaches to Berlin. The United States 9th Army already had crossed the Elbe River. In the Pacific, American forces were island-hopping toward Japan. When the vice president was escorted to the second floor of the White House, he found Eleanor waiting with her daughter and a White House assistant. Mrs. Roosevelt came up and put her arm on Mr. Truman's shoulder. "Harry," she said, "the President is dead."

By the time Mr. Truman took the oath of office that evening, critical areas of the world already had been transformed by war into new conditions that would, as a practical matter, stand beyond the power of an incoming President to change.

In the wake of the First World War, the second had fatally weakened the great European empires, notably the British Empire, which for decades had helped maintain a balance of power around the globe.

99

The once mighty nations of Germany and Japan were falling into ruins, creating enormous political vacuums in Asia and in the heart of Europe that would pose profound problems for the United States.

On the way to Germany the Red Army had overrun Poland; Soviet influence was extending a grip on Eastern Europe.

It had been arranged that the victorious American, French, British, and Soviet forces would occupy particular zones in Germany after the surrender. By April 12, 1945, the boundaries of those zones had been set by international agreement.

When Truman became President, therefore, the postwar world already has assumed certain forms that he would more or less have to live with.

Furthermore, he had stepped into a situation in which, as the time for postwar settlements approached, tensions and deep differences of outlook already had developed between the Western Allies, on the one hand and the Soviet Union, on the other, conflicts that a year or so later were to be referred to as the Cold War. The differences may not have been irremedial in 1945, but they were very serious, centering at first on the political future of Poland and disagreements between the Kremlin and the West as to the meaning of decisons made by Franklin D. Roosevelt, Joseph Stalin, and Winston Churchill at the Yalta Conference of February 1945.

Even before Truman assumed office certain recriminations had taken place between Roosevelt and Stalin. As victory approached, prewar suspicions between the Communist East and the Capitalist West were breaking through the wartime alliance against Hitler. The Roosevelt administration had begun backing away from a postwar loan to Stalin. Congressional opinion was hardening against further aid to the Soviets under Lend-Lease, the vehicle for providing America's allies with weapons and industrial equipment. Roosevelt had agreed with Churchill to keep from Stalin the secret that an atomic bomb was being developed in the United States.

As vice president in the eighty-three days before Roosevelt's death and as a senator before that, Truman had been kept utterly in the dark about the secrets of wartime diplomacy and strategy. He did not even have any exact knowledge that an atomic bomb was being built. He stepped into the White House at that crucial time with no experience whatever in the conduct of foreign affairs. He had never even met Churchill and the other allied war leaders.

Yet in the next nearly eight years Truman was to make, one after another, a series of momentous foreign policy decisions, some of which still affect our role in the world today. Through its foreign policy, the Truman administration marked a turning point in American history. I am not arguing that all that was done was for the best. There is still a good deal of debate on that question. But the results were profound and lasting. That is why Truman is important in history.

Inevitably, the questions arises: What was the critical, underlying, formative condition of the Truman administration? What made it possible for Truman to achieve the major initiatives that he undertook? What enabled a new President who was a novice in diplomacy and a political figure without any national following when he took office to lead the country in directions that would have seemed unimaginable only a few years earlier?

The condition that made all of that possible, it appears to me, was the remarkable and broad consensus on foreign policy that emerged in the United States at the close of the Second World War. It was a bipartisan consensus. It favored containment of Soviet expansion.

It has been said that Truman was ineffective because he could not get most of his Fair Deal domestic reforms through Congress. That may be true, but, basically, many of the reforms already had been legislated under Roosevelt. Truman, especially by his victory over Thomas E. Dewey in 1948, was able to preserve those reforms against heavy Republican assault.

The more important fact is that in nearly eight years of historic activity in foreign affairs Truman never lost a single major piece of foreign policy legislation in Congress. Moreover, all of those signal victories were won with votes to spare, even while the Republicans were in control of the 80th Congress of 1947 and 1948.

The measures and the foreign policy they projected were interventionist beyond anything the American people had ever dreamed of in times of peace in the past—interventionist in a historically isolationist country. And President Truman hailed from Missouri in the heart of what had been the most isolationist part of the nation—the Midwest. During the Truman administration both of Missouri's senators, Forrest C. Donnell and James P. Kem, voted against United States participation in the North Atlantic Treaty. Senator Kem voted against the Truman Doctrine and the Marshall Plan. Kem and Donnell were Republicans. In the prewar and postwar years it was the Republican party that was the stronghold of isolationism. As a young man, the son of fervent Democrats, Truman was deeply and lastingly influenced by Woodrow Wilson. Truman became a firm believer in the idea of the League of Nations. Through his reading indeed he had been attracted to the ideal of an international organization—a "Parliament of man," a "Federation of the world"—even before Wilson became President in 1913.

When Truman first entered the United States Senate in 1935, powerful currents already were running against American involvement in any war that might erupt around Hitler. As a freshman senator Truman did yield for a time to isolationist argument, growing out of the Senate munitions investigation, that bankers and munitions makers had maneuvered the United States into the First World War. In the isolationist tide he voted for the Neutrality Act. But as events continued to unfold in Europe and Asia, Truman turned against isolationism. Roosevelt's influence was undoubtedly a large factor. After Pearl Harbor, Truman favored Roosevelt's war aims, prominent among which, of course, was the founding of the United Nations and American participation in it.

Thus, as President, Truman came naturally to the foreign policy consensus that was to fall his lot to lead. Doubtless, some of his oft-criticized anti-Communist rhetoric in the White House was intended, consciously or otherwise, to preserve the consensus.

Two and a half months after Truman took office, the Senate provided a foretaste of what was coming when it approved American membership in the United Nations by a vote of 89 to 2. When you recall the League of Nations fight in the Senate in the Wilson administration and Franklin Roosevelt's bitter struggles with the isolationists on the eve of the Second World War, the consensus that emerged in favor of America's playing a dominant role in the world, beginning in 1945, was a remarkable development. I wish there were time to trace it in detail, but time permits only a look at the landmarks.

There was, of course, the deep fear aroused in this country by Hitler and Stalin. In this connection, there was the so-called lesson of Munich, the conviction that isolationism and appeasement only led to war. There was Roosevelt's skill in ultimately winning public acceptance of his war aims. Probably the patriotic support for unconditional surrender was a factor in building the consensus. There was also the veritable earthquake in the Republican party in 1940 that routed the isolationists and produced the nomination of the internationalist-minded Wendell L. Willkie. There was the strong support of many leading newspapers for the ideal of collective security after the Second World War. There was the significant, as it proved to be, switch from isolationism to internationalism by Senator Arthur H. Vandenberg, Republican, of Michigan, who was to become chairman of the Senate Foreign Relations Committee at a crucial time.

There was the powerful influence of men like General George C. Marshall and Dean Acheson and, yes, General Dwight D. Eisenhower and John Foster Dulles, who negotiated the Japanese peace treaty for Truman. It is worth remembering that the consensus did not only bring together Republicans and Democrats. It also brought together civilians and the military leaders, who wielded great influence at the close of the war.

Some of you may recall the bitter troubles that Truman had over China policy in contrast to European policy and may wonder, therefore, about the scope of the consensus. In very large measure the dispute over China policy sprang from domestic politics—from the opportunity that the Republican right wing saw to pillory Truman and the Democratic party over the Communist seizure of China in 1949. In truth, Truman and the mainstream of the Republican party were not so far apart on China as the controversy made it seem.

Truman did not want the Communists to take control of China any more than the Republicans did. He simply could not conceive of any way in which the United States could at reasonable cost change the historic process that was under way in China. The proof that the American people did not want to become involved in a war in China to try to save Chiang Kai-shek and the Nationalist regime was amply demonstrated by the failure of General Douglas MacArthur to overturn Truman's policy during the Korean War.

The Truman period was indeed filled more often than not with raging controversy. Unlike the differences thundering around domestic questions, Truman, in matters of foreign policy, found himself aligned with powerful groups in banks, in the large law firms, in the universities, in the press, in organized labor, in Congress, and in the government bureaucracies, civilian and military. The consensus made the historic foreign policy initiatives possible, which is, to me at least, the fundamental fact about the Truman presidency.

One of the most extraordinary consequences of the Second World War was that it not only doomed the old empires but brought about the rise of two superpowers, the United States and the Soviet Union. As I mentioned, Truman took office at the very time when tensions between these two powers was becoming serious. All his major foreign policy decisions were made against the backdrop of that ever-increasing rivalry and the anti-Communist sentiment it fanned in the United States.

So much has been said about the origins of the Cold War that I do not want to dwell upon the question now. For whatever it may be worth, I take a middle-of-the-road view, siding neither with those who put all the blame on the Soviet Union nor with those who put all the blame on the United States. The trouble, it seems to me, arose out of the interaction between the interests, traditions, cultures, political systems, and national security policies of the two superpowers.

At a time of nearly global upheaval, the United States viewed the Soviets as imposing their will on Eastern Europe and probing ominously in the Balkans and the Middle East. For their part, the Soviets, with their memories of Allied intervention in the First World War, feared that if the capitalist nations were to dominate Eastern Europe, they might exploit it as a hostile base against the Soviet Union. Old fears of revolutionary Communism were reawakening in the West, matching the suspicion and zenophobia in Moscow.

In the political vacuum created in the heart of Europe by the defeat of Germany, an anticapitalist nation and an anti-Communist nation began to converge and compete, each having aspirations for world leadership. Mistrust became pervasive. And into the witches' brew came the atomic bomb, first as an American monopoly and then as a weapon in the hands of each of the adversaries.

At the outset, Truman took a generally cautious course with respect to Stalin. Month by month, however, the American position hardened as a result of the dismay caused in Washington by Stalin's tightening grip on Poland and Eastern Europe and his probing for influence in the Black Sea Straits and in Iran. In Febraury 1946 the Truman adminstration and the American public were stunned by disclosure that a Soviet spy ring had been operating in Ottawa to get information on the American atomic bomb.

Into this heated atmosphere on February 22, 1946, came a cable from George F. Kennan, American charge d'affaires in Moscow, portraying Soviet policy as dynamically expansionist and thus a threat to American interests. The cable added, however, that Soviet power usually backed off "when strong resistance is encountered at any point."

The message had the effect of crystallizing the thinking of the administration and turning it toward what became its ultimate policy: the policy of containment of international Communism emanating from the Soviet Union and, in time, from Red China.

A great landmark in postwar foreign policy was passed in 1947 with the pronouncement of the Truman Doctrine and the furnishing of military and economic aid to Greece and Turkey, both of which felt themselves menaced by Soviet pressure. Up to that point Greece and Turkey had received military and economic support from Great Britain, but the British economy, unable to rally from the ravages of the war, was all but paralyzed. The British government asked the United

States to assume the burden of insuring the independence of Greece and Turkey. In fact, that was a logical step in the direction in which the administration already had been moving to contain Soviet expansion.

Truman accepted the advice of his secretary of state, George C. Marshall, and the then under secretary of state, Dean Acheson, that he ask Congress for $400,000,000 for assistance to Greece and Turkey. Critical historians later said that the danger of Soviet intervention in Greece or Turkey was exaggerated. Nevertheless, the fear in Washington was strong at the time, partly because of the belief that, if the Soviets could control Greece and Turkey, they could also dominate the Middle East, with worldwide consequences.

Actually, two concepts in Washington were taking shape simultaneously. One was the Greek-Turkish aid program, which came to be called the Truman Doctrine because of the sweeping terms that the President broached it to Congress. The other was a program for massive economic assistance to all of Western Europe, which became know as the Marshall Plan, named for the secretary of state. Truman called the concepts "two halves of the same walnut."

As the drafting of the Truman Doctrine speech proceeded under Acheson's supervision, it grew ever bolder and more far-reaching. When President Truman appeared before a joint session of Congress on March 12, 1947, he said, "I believe it must be the policy of the United States to support free peoples who are resisting attempted subjugation by armed minorities or by outside pressures." No geographical limits were mentioned. Truman said "all peoples." That was the epitome of containment.

Aid to Greece and Turkey passed Congress with relative ease. To the best of my recollection, the Truman Doctrine was far less controversial then than it became during the Vietnam War. In the controversy of the 1960s historians, particularly younger ones, began to read back through the documents to determine what could have led us into the detestable war in Southeast Asia. It did not take long for their eyes to alight on the passage in the Truman Doctrine that it must be the policy of the United States to support free people who were resisting subjugation by armed minorities or by outside pressures. To some of the inquiring historians, therefore, the Truman Doctrine was seen as the root cause of the American disaster in Vietnam.

To be sure, even the Truman administration did not apply the doctrine universally. A frequently cited omission was China, where the United States made no really major effort to prevent the Chinese Communists from seizing control of the recognized Nationalist government. Furthermore subsequent Presidents, including Kennedy and

Johnson, who materially increased the American commitment in Vietnam, were not bound to follow a policy enunciated by President Truman. On the other hand, there can be little doubt but what the Truman Doctrine gave a certain enduring coloration to American foreign policy. By applying containment, it influenced future American actions down the line, probably to Vietnam. It may in the process have lent a rigidity to American policy that inhibited a turn from the Cold War.

The Marshall Plan for economic aid came next. It was occasioned by two conditions primarily. One was the rocklike impasse prevailing between the United States and the Soviet Union over a settlement of European problems. The other was the failure of the Western European economy to recover from the devastation and dislocation of the war. On the one hand, the United States feared that, especially in Italy and France, economic disintegration might lead to political collapse, opening the way for Communists to seize control in Rome and Paris. On the other hand, there was apprehension that by gaining control of Germany and Austria the Soviets might wed the great resources and industrial plants of the vital center of Europe to those of the Soviet Union itself, thereby creating an overpowering and hostile block.

One of the great purposes of the Marshall Plan, therefore, was to rebuild Europe economically to buttress it against the perceived danger of Communist inroads. By the standards of the day, the Marshall Plan was a huge long-range undertaking estimated to cost $15 billion. Much of that money would be spent for supplies produced in the United States. Hence a strong selling point for the plan was that it would be good for American business and industry. And it was. No one who covered the Marshall Plan debates in Congress, as I did, however, could ignore the fact that there was also a substantial element of generosity and willingness to help allies who were in trouble. While the Marshall Plan is often criticized as a tool of the Cold War, it has also been widely hailed as a noble undertaking. Its beneficial effect on conditions in Western Europe was obvious. I was in the infantry during the Second World War and I left Europe in 1945 seeing it then in indescribable shambles. I went back there for my first postwar visit maybe 15 years later and what had happened to Europe was unbelievable. You would hardly have known there was a war there.

Bear in mind that the underlying reason for extending massive economic, and later military aid to Europe was that Europe was viewed by American policymakers as the core of the civilization of which the United States was a part. To revive the strength and vitality of Europe, to restore its polity, culture, economy, finances, trade, cities, and farms was considered essential to the continuing health and prosperity of the United States itself.

Those considerations produced the basic premise of Truman's foreign policy, as they had produced the fundamental premise of Roosevelt's. That premise was that in the matter of American national security Europe took precedence over Asia, even when the Communists were seizing control of China and even when war was raging in Korea.

The American course in Europe after the Second World War was studded with major and far-reaching decisions. Indeed they were so numerous I can only sketch the main outlines.

Defeated Germany was divided into four zones of occupation, one each for the United States, Great Britain, and France in the western area of Germany and one for the Soviets in the eastern half of Germany. The eventual goal was a reunited and disarmed Germany. As we see today, Germany never was reunited. The obstruction of this goal began with the French, who had had their fill of a powerful and united Germany and vetoed almost any step that might have led to centralized authority in occupied Germany.

With the Cold War settling in, differences quickly developed between the Allies in their Western zones and the Soviets in the East. Among the most serious issues, the Allies would not permit the Soviets to share in the control of the industrially important Ruhr Valley in Western Germany, nor would the Allies allow the Soviets to extract the amount of reparations that the Kremlin demanded from the Western zones of occupation.

Washington reacted against the taking of large Soviet reparations from the American zone because it would retard economic recovery there and thus burden American taxpayers with the cost of occupation. Because of the German economic plight, the Americans and British in time merged their zones of occupation. The French zone eventually joined the merger. Therefore there was one Allied zone in the West and a Soviet zone in the East.

In 1948, two alarming events hastened the division of Europe between the Democratic West and the Communist East. The first event was the Communist seizure of Czechoslovakia, a crisis that caused a far worse shock in America then than was felt over recent events in Poland. The British and French took the lead in agitating for a new defense system that a year later materialized in the North Atlantic Treaty. The second frightening event was the Soviet land blockade of the Allied zones in Berlin—an act interpreted in Washington as a move to force the United States out of Germany, if not out of Europe.

General Lucius D. Clay, commandant of the United States occupation zone, wanted to push a military convoy through to Berlin to challenge a Soviet blockade. Truman overruled the proposal for fear it might trigger a war with the Soviet Union. Instead, he approved an airlift to supply the Allied zones in Berlin indefinitely. He also approved a counter-blockade against the Soviet zone in Berlin. By May 1949 these measures broke the Soviet blockade of the German capital.

By then, drastic change was on the way. The blockade had utterly wrecked what was left of four-power control of Germany. The West already had taken steps to integrate the occupied zones of West Germany into the economy of Western Europe. Now a movement began to establish an independent West German government on the territory of the American, British, and French zones. Soon, a new German Republic was formed as part of a political and ultimately a military alliance with the Western powers, although the actual rearming of West Germany did not begin until the Eisenhower adminstration.

The Soviets reacted by establishing the Peoples Democratic Republic in their zone. Before the end of the Truman administration, therefore, two Germanys existed in the heart of Europe in political, economic, and ideological conflict with each other, the one supported by the United States and its allies, the other by the Soviet Union.

The dangerous tensions convinced Allied leaders in Europe and America that the Marshall Plan might not be enough to save Western Europe from a Soviet attack. What was needed, in their view, was a military shield behind which Western Europe would have a chance to regain its strength under the stimulus of the Marshall Plan. This conviction—strong on both sides of the Atlantic—produced the North Atlantic Treaty, signed on April 4, 1949. For the United States the milestone that was passed that day was the policy of no permanent alliances outside the Western Hemisphere, which had been followed practically since George Washington's Farewell Address. The Treaty, declaring that an attack on any one of the signatories was to be considered an attack on all, was the very end of the old isolationism. Truman did what no other President had ever done when he stationed American combat troops in Europe in peacetime.

If Europe had priority, Asia was the source of Harry Truman's deepest troubles. Basically, the cause was the triumph of Mao Zedong's Communist forces in the Chinese civil war. Unlike the great questions in Europe, the China problem created severe political stress in the United States because the conservative wing of the Republican party fervently supported the Chinese Nationalists, led by Chiang Kai-shek. The domestic political controversy eroded Truman's leadership.

China, for example, was to become a major factor in the rise and dismaying success of the red-baiting Senator Joseph R. MacCarthy. Abroad, the China issue caused difficulties among the United States and its traditional allies. At home, it provoked bitter quarrels within the administration itself, particularly over the collateral question of the status of Taiwan, or Formosa, as it was then called.

Speaking now of China. Roosevelt's policy, which Truman inherited and tried to carry on, was to recognize the Chiang Kai-shek regime as the legitimate government of China and to deal with it and not with the Communists. By the time Truman took office, however, Chiang's was already the dying order and Mao's the new order. Truman began, therefore, by backing the losing side in the Chinese civil war. It would in fact have been politically out of the question for him even if he hadn't felt bound to follow Roosevelt policies suddenly to have switched allegiance to the Communists.

The consequences of the mounting Chinese Communist victories against Chiang Kai-shek were enormous. The Truman administration, for example, was fearful that in the end Mao's forces would sweep southward not only into all of mainland China but into Indochina as well. In Vietnam, at the heart of Indochina, another civil war was already being waged between the forces of Ho Chi Minh and French colonial troops. France had ruled Indochina for more than half a century. Displaced by Japanese forces furing the Second World War, the French had returned and were trying to restore their old position. An insurrection in Vietnam had been rallied under the banner of Ho Chi Minh, a Vietnamese nationalist and Communist. In opposition to Ho, France set up a puppet regime under Bao Dai, a former emperor in the region. Desperate to keep Indochina out of Communist hands, the Truman administration decided early in 1950 to give the Bao Dai regime economic and military support. It was only to be a matter of weeks, however, before the first escalation of American assistance to the anti-Communist forces took place. Thus, as the Pentagon Papers were to say, the United States in 1950 had become "directly involved in the developing tragedy of Vietnam." Truman had taken the first grave step in an American commitment to prevent the consequences of what came to be called in the Eisenhower administration "the domino theory."

Another major effect of the crumbling of Chiang Kai-shek's Nationalists was a major shift in American focus toward Japan. A friendly Japan rather than a Communist China loomed as a more likely partner for the United States in the maintenance of stability—and containment—in Asia. Unremarked at the time, the drift toward partnership with Japan was bound to affect the strategic importance of nearby Korea. Truman approved a policy in 1949 of supporting an economically strong Japan (only a few years prior to that time our bitter enemy).

On October 1, 1949, Mao proclaimed the Peoples Republic of China, and soon Chiang fled to Taiwan. The question was posed, therefore, as to whether Truman would recognize the new Communist regime in Mainland China. A decision of great importance. Considerable political pressure in Congress and in the press was exerted against recognition, and the Chinese Communists were just belligerent enough to make recognition difficult for Truman. He temporized. Essentially, however, his aim was to grant recognition to the Communist regime as soon as it seemed in the American interest to do so. If things had gone along on a fairly even keel, he might well have recognized the Communist regime after the 1950 congressional elections in the United States.

Things did not go on an even keel. On June 25, 1950, the Soviet-supported forces of North Korea invaded American supported South Korea. Swiftly, Truman committed American forces to what was to become the third largest foreign war in American history up to that time to repulse the Communist invaders.

In a nutshell, the Korean situation was this:

Since 1910 Korea had been under Japanese rule. When Japan surrendered after the dropping of two atomic bombs in August 1945, American and Soviet forces both entered Korea to protect their own interests and to supervise the repatriation of Japanese soldiers. The Soviets occupied northern Korea, the Americans, southern Korea. The dividing line was the 38th parallel. As in Germany, the plan was for the two occupying powers to stabilize the country, arrange for elections, and then withdraw, leaving an independent self-governing Korea. As in Germany, the Americans and the Soviets developed their own zone according to their own interests and could not agree on terms for unification of the country. Eventually, mutually hostile independent governments were created in the north and the south, the latter, at American instigation, under the aegis of the United Nations. Then the Americans and the Soviets withdrew, leaving their respective clients at each other's throats across the 38th parallel. Tension built until June 1950 when the North Koreans perceived a chance to win a quick victory, and marched across the parallel intending to bring all of Korea under Communist rule.

That prospect threatened one more humiliation that Truman was not willing to accept. The Communists had seized Czechoslovakia to swell their empire in Eastern Europe. The Communists had seized

China, which the United States had sought as its own ally in Asia. The preceding September—September 1949—the Soviets had exploded a nuclear device, ending the American monopoly on the atomic bomb. Throughout the Far East indigenous Communist forces were stirring up trouble in Burma, Indonesia, and the Philippines as well as in Vietnam. Soviet Communism and Chinese Communism had taken on the appearance of an enormous monolithic force. And now a Communist attack in Korea seemed to point a dagger at Japan, then America's main bastion in the Orient. The North Korean invasion set off in the United States an almost universal cry for drawing the line against further Communist advance. That is precisely what Truman decided to do, motivated also by two other major considerations. One was that, having involved the United Nations in the birth of South Korea, Truman felt that he could not stand by and permit the United Nations to be defied, lest the organization disintegrate like the League of Nations after the Italian invasion of Ethiopia. The other consideration was that the British capitulation to Hitler at Munich had taught Truman and his advisers that appeasement only whets the appetite of an aggressor. In other words, Truman feared that if the Communists could get away with the attack in Korea, they might then assault the Middle East or Europe. As he understood the lesson of Munich, the right time to halt aggression was the first time.

So, with global consequences, the battle for Korea was joined. As one of the first steps in committing American forces Truman stationed the Seventh Fleet in the Strait of Formosa to prevent Chiang Kai-shek's forces from attempting an invasion of the mainland from Taiwan and to prevent the Chinese Communists troops from invading Taiwan. Either movement might have caused the Korean War to spread, which Truman was trying to prevent. The positioning of the American fleet in the Formosan Strait, however, dangerously alarmed the Chinese Communists about their own security. Truman also increased economic and military assistance to Vietnam, deepening the American commitment there, though he never sent any combat troops to Indochina.

American troops in Korea, heavily outnumbered at first, barely hung on after the initial commitment to battle. But in less than three months, they drove the Communist invaders back across the 38th parallel. In Washington those summer months of 1950 were a time of critical decisions.

The ease with which Communist forces had driven into South Korea had made it appallingly clear to Truman and his advisers how easily Soviet troops might move westward through Germany to the English

Channel. Only the United States had the military potential to protect and to arm the NATO powers, but after the Second World War American conventional military forces had been cut to the bone in a pell mell demobilization.

In the months following the Soviet nuclear test the national security establishment in Washington reviewed the nation's strategic position. In a famous document designated NSC 68 it urged a vast program to rearm not only the United States but its principal allies. During the spring of 1950 Truman marked time on the proposal. After the Korean invasion with its attendant fears of a possible Soviet invasion of Europe or the Middle East, he approved NSC 68. His decision moved the country in a direction that is all too familiar to us today. In the fiscal year 1950, which ended just after the Korean war began, the total budget for defense and international affairs was $17.7 billion. For the fiscal year 1951, first full year of the Korean War, the total rose to $53.4 billion and has pretty much been rising steadily since. As part of the whole development, talks were begun on the eventual rearmament of Germany, and Truman dispatched combat troops to Europe, where they are stationed still.

In the fall of 1950 Truman made a momentous decision in the dilemma that was posed by the retreat of the North Koreans to the 38th parallel, leaving the North Koreans free to resume the war when they were ready again. Should Truman, risking hostilities with China or the Soviet Union, authorize General Douglas MacArthur to cross the parallel to destroy the North Korean army once and for all and thus dispose of the Korean problem?

To halt was to ensure loud dissatisfaction at home with an inglorious outcome that left the Communists still in power in North Korea and American troops stationed indefinitely in South Korea, securing the parallel. To proceed was to seize a rare opportunity to roll back the Communist orbit in Asia to the borders of China and the Soviet Union, realizing the grandest dreams of containment.

The war aim of the United States when Truman committed the forces in Korea was to compel the invaders to withdraw to the 38th parallel. As far as it went, that would have been a notable achievement, which also would have enhanced the ideal of collective security through the United Nations. But the issue was not simple, for the long-standing objective of the United States and the United Nations was to promote the establishment of a free, independent, and united Korea. And the destruction of the North Korean army could have opened the way to that goal. There was, too, a danger that the South Korean army, also fighting under MacArthur, would not agree to halt and would march across the parallel on its own initiative to finish off the North Korean foe. In America, public sentiment for a final solution in Korea was rising. Republicans were pressing for a victorious drive to the north and threatening to make an issue of it in the forthcoming November 1950 congressional elections if a chance for victory were not seized. And furthermore, there was this incentive too. If Truman had marched north in Korea and unified Korea, unquestionably it would have been regarded as a great achievement of his administration.

For a complex of reasons Truman ordered MacArthur to cross the 38th parallel to destroy the North Korean forces. MacArthur was authorized, if need be, to advance all the way to the Yalu River, the boundary between Korea and China. Uneasy about the presence of the American fleet in the Strait of Formosa and newly worried over the threat of MacArthur's pending drive toward Manchuria, the Chinese Communist government stated in various ways that China would intervene if American forces crossed the thirty-eighth parallel. The warning did not move Washington. MacArthur's orders were not changed. On November 24, 1950 MacArthur was on hand for the great offensive. "If this operation is successful," he said, "I hope we can get the boys home for Christmas." Neither he nor any other American authority knew that three hundred thousand Chinese soldiers had secretly infiltrated the mountains and forests of northern Korea and were poised to spring.

The upshot, as you know, was a ghastly rout of the Allied forces, a bitter retreat in ice and snow back across the 38th parallel. Indeed the United States 10th Corps was very nearly trapped before it could be evacuated by sea.

An appalling consequence of the new conflict was that for the next twenty years Communist China and the United States were implacable enemies. Indeed it was largely out of fear of China that Presidents Eisenhower, Kennedy, Johnson, and Nixon escalated the commitment that President Truman had first made to help keep Vietnam out of Communist hands.

The Chinese onslaught in Korea also precipitated a classic showdown in the history of American foreign policy. By mid-January, 1951, the Allied forces had finally stemmed the Chinese sweep in the area of the 38th parallel. But there the fighting was stabilized. By that time the United States and its allies had agreed not to make another attempt to conquer North Korea. That decision was anathema to General MacArthur, who found it intolerable to end his great career in stalemate. The United States, he maintained, was in a new war and should act accordingly, blockading the Chinese coast and bombing its industrial centers.

In one of his last cardinal decisions in foreign policy Truman rejected MacArthur's proposals and insisted on keeping the war limited to South Korea. MacArthur defied the President, and Truman relieved him of his command.

A number of compelling reasons lay behind Truman's decision. China and the Soviet Union were partners in a non-aggression pact. An attack on China, therefore, might have involved the United States in hostilities with both of those powers—in short in a third world war. Even a blockade of the China coast, if it were to be effective, might have involved blockading the Soviet port of Vladivostok, an act of war against the Soviets. In a widened war Soviet and Chinese air power might have threatened our troops in Korea by destroying airfields and choking the already crowded ports in South Korea and Japan. If the United States were going to get into war with the Soviet Union, Asia was not the battlefield it preferred. Finally, and compellingly, the United States in 1951 was not prepared for war with China let alone with the Soviet Union.

THE TRUMAN PRESIDENCY AND THE FOREIGN POLICY PROCESS
Lucius Battle

MR. THOMPSON: I'd like to welcome you to a Forum with the Honorable Lucius Battle. Anyone who has followed foreign policy at all carefully in recent Democratic administrations knows of the very central and responsible role that Luke Battle has played. He was special assistant from 1949 to 1953 to Secretary of State Dean Acheson. He toured the world with Mr. Acheson and attended all the major conferences in that period. He was special assistant to Secretary of State Dean Rusk from 1961 to 1964. Sandwiched in between these high and important posts were such significant roles as ambassador to the United Arab Republic; assistant secretary for Education and Cultural Affairs; assistant secretary for South Asian and near Eastern Affairs; and a whole series of other roles in Washington such as executive secretary of the Department of State.

As one reviews his career it would seem that every time a Democratic administration has needed a key person to check and be sure that everything was getting done that ought to be done, they have called on Luke Battle.

He is a graduate of the University of Florida, AB and LLB; and he holds an honorary doctorate from Florida State. I'm sorry that Ray Frantz, our senior librarian at Alderman, is not present because he would have noted with pride that Luke Battle began his career as manager of the student staff for the University of Florida library.

He served as first secretary of the American Embassy in Copenhagan. He also served as vice president, then senior vice president, and then director of COMSAT.

He has been chairman of the Foreign Policy Institute of the School of Advanced International Studies of Johns Hopkins University since 1980. He was president of the Middle East Institute in the early seventies. Among numerous *pro-bono* activities, he was vice president of colonial Williamsburg; was a member of the Protestant Episcopal Catholic Foundation; was chairman of the board of St. Albans School; was a member of the Board of Directors of the Middle East Institute and the School for Advanced International Studies; a trustee of the George Marshall Foundation and of the American University in Cairo; and chairman of the Visiting Committee of the Harvard Center for Middle East Studies. He is a founding member of the Council of the Institute for the Study of Diplomacy, serving from 1978 to the present. He also served as lieutenant in the United States Navy from 1943 to 1946.

He has discussed the subject of the afternoon on BBC broadcasts and in other connections. We look forward to his discussion of the foreign policy process of the Truman presidency.

MR. BATTLE: Thank you very much. I have been getting recently quite a few invitations to speak on the Truman period, on General Marshall, on Dean Acheson, on various things. In addition to that I've done a number of hours with the BBC which are being carried now, some of them will be carried over here. I've said to everyone exactly the same thing—I was a very minor figure in the Truman era and I think it is a mistake to believe for one second that I was a major figure. I'm a good listener and I did happen to be present at a great many of the major events and the major incidents that occurred in that period. I traveled with Acheson and went to all the meetings and whatever. I was twenty-nine years old when that started. It was really the beginning of what became a very exciting career in the foreign service which I enjoyed very, very much.

Let's talk for a bit about the Truman era and some of the forces at work at this particularly interesting and incredible period in American history.

I found the era fascinating for a lot of reasons. I was very young. I found working for Dean Acheson extraordinary. He was a remarkable man, a most brilliant, positive, dynamic personality who became a very real and important force in my life. That really changed me totally. I think if I ever had a model it was Dean. We continued our friendship throughout his life. He was in many ways a kind of eighteenth century man. In twenty-five years when we weren't in the same town we wrote each other regularly, once or twice a week. And sometimes they were short notes and then they would run into fifteen or twenty or thirty pages. I have letters from him—stacks of letters—which I've let his son use. A few of them were in a book that David Acheson published called *Among Friends*. And here and there they have been used but I have never and would never draw from them myself for any purpose except perhaps to set records straight. They have a way of getting awfully mixed up these days.

Let's look to the period and the moment and the feeling. No one expected Harry Truman to win. Nobody contributed to the campaign. Therefore he came in office in a most unusual way. He had no commitments. He had no obligations. He didn't have to do anything. Myron Taylor had kept that train running and had written the checks as they ran out of coal or whatever trains burn. Myron Taylor didn't want anything except ambassador to the Vatican and he never got that. So it was a peculiar sort of situation but out of this particular thing emerged what became the American establishment, certainly in the field of foreign affairs. I have to talk about this largely in the realm of foreign affairs because that is my own area, the context in which I came in contact with President Truman and with Dean Acheson. But there were no obligations.

President Truman was very fond of Dean Acheson. Truman once told me that as the appointments were being made for his Cabinet that he had gotten down to three figures, Lewis Douglas, Averell Harriman, and Dean Acheson and he said he had selected Dean for one major reason and that was he had such a tremendous following on the Hill. Well, Congress of course became his *bête noir* before we were through with it. He got into a conflict on the Hill for ridiculous reasons. Nevertheless, at the time he was appointed, Dean had been assistant secretary for congressional affairs at one stage and he had particularly good relations on the Hill. They were rather intimidated. He was a startling figure. He did not suffer fools lightly. He was not intimidated. We were supposed to be intimidated by the Congress and he wasn't. That bothered him later but for awhile this was great. He managed to contain himself during those days in the earlier period and that went fairly well. It was later he began to have trouble.

At any rate, Dean was appointed secretary of state for those reasons, plus the fact he had been under secretary. He had had more experience in the field than probably anyone else. He was widely known to be a good loyal Trumanite. There were a lot of little incidents that many people tended to credit for the appointment. I don't know if this one is true but the story goes that when Mr. Truman rejoined the campaign no one expected it to go anywhere. Everyone thought Dewey was going to be President. And he came back to town on the train one night and nobody bothered to go out to meet him except Dean Acheson. None of the Cabinet, nobody went. But Dean showed up at the train and he was the only senior official from government. I forgot whether he went home with him or what but at any rate that gave a feeling of loyalty and devotion to Truman which continued throughout the Truman period.

Dean had been under secretary under General Marshall and had been out for a year before he came back as secretary. I met him during that period in a particular kind of a way. I was on the Canadian desk and he had a client in Canada; it had something to do with wood pulp. I was the bottom of the barrel in the Office of European Affairs. Faced with this issue of wood pulp in Canada, Dean came in. He was out of office and was representing a client. He went to see the assistant secretary for European Affairs under whom Canada, as part of the British Commonwealth, was located organizationally. The assistant secretary had never heard of the problem and they got to the deputy who had never heard of it and they got the next man. By the time I got there the room was full. I was the bottom of the barrel but I was the only one who had ever read the telegrams or anything about it. So he asked me what I thought of this particular problem and I said I think A, B, and C and D and he said, "Well, young man, I want to tell you that our Ambassador to Canada is my house guest and he says he disagrees with everything you've said." I said, "Well, Mr. Secretary, he's entitled to his view and I'm entitled to mine. I think he's wrong." I thought, this has finished this little relationship. Months went by, I don't remember the issue but I was proved right.

When he became secretary of state he asked for a bachelor he could work to death. He said, "It's enough to think about my own family, I don't want to think about my assistant's family and my staff's family. Make up a list of bachelors whom I can work to death." So they got about four or five bachelors in the Department of State and since my name begins with a B, I was first on the list. He never interviewed the rest. I walked in the room and he said, "I remember you." I was terrified he would. And he said, "You've got a lot of courage." He said,

"How would you like to work for me?" I said, "I would be delighted." He said, "Can you start tomorrow?" I said, "Certainly." So I left the Canadian desk and never went back to reality again.

But from then on a lot of things happened and I think these were interesting in a number of contexts and partly reflect the nature of the Truman thing.

In these days when the relationship between the White House staff and the Department of State become such a topic of major discussion I think it is interesting to note my first entry into that particular realm. The secretary took me over to meet the President which I thought was very generous of him, very kind. I was very junior but close to the top of the department. However, I was not a senior official. So I was taken to meet the President. I thought that was great.

A couple of days later I got a call from that famous General Vaughan, a poker-playing friend of President Truman's, and he said, "A paper is about to come up in the Department of State recommending course A and I hope the secretary will not approve that paper. Tell him that. I hope he will buy course B." So I waited until the paper came up and I went in to see the secretary with the paper and I said, "I have this document for your approval and we've had a call from Harry Vaughan and he says he hopes that we will accept course B." And he said, "What do you think, Luke?" I said, "I think course A is the right course. You've got the problem with the White House and Harry Vaughan." He looked at me and he said, "When Harry Vaughan calls you don't even go to the telephone. If he gives you any trouble of any kind we will speak to the President about it." He said, "Don't ever tell me what Harry Vaughan or anybody else over there thinks. Tell me what you think but don't tell me what they think. It's unimportant."

Now that's what set the relationship. And it was typical. There was a very small White House staff. In sharp contrast, I have to tell you this rather amusing story. I went back to government when President Kennedy came in. I went back to the secretary's office for about a year to help Dean Rusk get started. The first day I was in that office, the administration was full of all sorts of people who either had big names or thought they had or were trying to arrive. They were fine but I hadn't been in the office ten minutes when Dean Rusk said to me, "Luke, will you please try to place our relations with the White House staff on a different basis? You know all those fellows. It's impossible! They are coming into the department at all kinds of levels and the President is getting recommendations that have no coordination and no relationship to what the Department of State thinks." It was a sharp contrast from the past. It got even worse later with Mac Bundy and all those people. I took a particularly dim view of Brzezinski but—I'm off the course now.

It did seem to me that in terms of the way government operated, particularly the White House staff versus the Cabinet, that the Truman era was the best era I have been involved in over all the years I have been in and out of government. I believe that this ability to foster cooperation was one of the great strengths of Truman. He had other strengths; he was wise, though he was not terribly well educated in a formal sense, but he was an avid reader. He read all the time and he knew a lot. There was a sense of humility about him that let him to pick the best Cabinet that we'd had around town for a very long time. It really was the best Cabinet we've ever had; it was a bipartisan Cabinet and there were very few political obligations growing out of financial contributions to the 1948 campaign. In that period there came forward many who became major figures. The group cut across party lines completely and served all sorts of administrations: Bob Lovett, Jack McCloy, General Marshall, Paul Hoffman, Averell Harriman, and Bill Foster. There were as many Republicans in the names I just mentioned as there were Democrats. So this was a remarkable quality about it. They had some bad people, too. I thought Louis Johnson was a disaster; I thought John Snyder was weak. There were a lot of people I did not consider terribly distinguished but *in toto* the Cabinet looks, in today's world, remarkably good.

The nation was emerging for the first time as an international power. We had put isolation behind us. We were groping for a positon in the world that we thought we wanted. We had oversold the UN. Everyone believed for a while that if you had the UN everything was solved and there was no problem from then on. That was very untrue. The realities of East/West relations were beginning to scare and sober us. We had just disarmed, and the fact that we could go back, that we could talk about rearming, all of those things were shocking to us. We recognized the NATO treaty was almost completely negotiated just before the Truman era began. I sat in on the last few weeks of the negotiations on that treaty. It was a remarkable group of ambassadors to Washington. All of them had known each other fairly well: Henri Bonnet of France, Britain's Oliver Franks—all of them very close friends. It was a wonderful example of how negotiations should be and can be conducted. Out of it emerged the treaty which was signed in April of 1949 putting us on a new course. But the big event, the big thing was the Marshall Plan. And that was truly a new direction.

It is interesting that with all the troubles that Truman and Acheson got into on the Hill, they never failed to get what they wanted and that was astonishing. At the same time they were seeking bigger and bigger appropriations for aid to Europe, military assistance and military programs which Louis Johnson bitterly opposed in the beginning. Later he departed and Marshall took over. In spite of all that Truman and Acheson were still being accused of being soft on Communism. All sorts of outrageous statements were being made. But nevertheless, the appropriations were granted. They got through what they tried to get through. They got all their programs approved. It was remarkable. We went through some really rather perilous times.

The Korean War: I think we will still be talking about this one, arguing about what caused it or whether it could have been avoided for many years to come. The finger usually points to Dean Acheson's Press Club speech. In his talk he drew a perimeter in which he said there was a line and on this side, if there is an attack, we will respond immediately, directly and unilaterally, hoping to bring others in with us. Then there was a line here where, if crossed, we would go to the UN, etc. The speech had quite a history. He made it from notes. Dean Rusk, Walt Butterworth, and I stayed at his house until nearly 2:00 in the morning. He had the speech the next day at noon. We were being accused of having no Far East policy, no China policy. Chiang Kai-shek's fall left a terrible vacuum. There was no attention given to the perimeter.

The Korean War is interesting. We went in on June 25, 1950 on Sunday. The strange thing is at the very beginning of the Korean War it was an enormously popular war. I remember talking to John Foster Dulles and I want to come back to Mr. Dulles and his role in a number of ways. Dulles was in Japan when the actual fighting started and he came right back, he was not involved with the decision at all particularly at the beginning of the war. He said, "This has made the UN into a living vital thing." The leaders of Congress said to the President and to Dean Acheson, "We can get a joint resolution endorsing what's been done. There is no problem at all." President Truman said, "No." He did not want that. He said, "There is no question about public support for it and I do not want to weaken the power of the presidency." The President must be able to respond in actions of this kind. By that time, the United Nations had backed him, not as much as I would have hoped but in terms of troops. They had given him political support and there was a fair response, though not great.

The war was very popular until the weekend of December 2, 1950. After the great march to the Yalu River, it looked as though all of American power was totally committed to a war to which there was no end. It could be a disaster. That weekend it became very unpopular.

Everyone began to call it "Truman's War" and the whole thing changed. We can argue endlessly about what went wrong. The orders that went to MacArthur involved one of the few real fights I ever had with Dean Acheson. At the time, we were in New York at the UN. Dean Rusk had cleared the instructions to MacArthur. The Inchon landing had occurred. It had been a sensational success. There had been serious doubt in the military as to whether MacArthur could pull it off and he did. He did it brilliantly. But then the question came as to what happened next. Instructions had to be given and the press was saying that we were holding him back from crossing the thirty-eighth parallel and we were not trying to win the war. The same issues came up, of course, in Vietnam.

The instructions came from Washington—to New York—they were brought up by Dean Rusk, a long telegram for clearance. The secretary was busy so I went over the telegram while Dean Rusk was sitting just outside the door. I took it in with Dean Rusk, who was then assistant secretary of state of the Far East. Acheson read it and I said, "I don't think these orders are clear. They leave it entirely up to him, to MacArthur, to his judgment as to how far he goes and what he does. You don't want to leave that man free." Acheson got furious with me. He said, "How old are you?" I said, "I'm thirty." He said, "Would you be willing to take on the whole Joint Chiefs of Staff and say that they are wrong and you are right?" I said, "Those instructions *are not clear!*" And they weren't clear. They are published in Acheson's book *Present at the Creation*. I felt that then and have said it many times since then. They left it up to the general totally. And it seems to me that that brought forth absolute disaster.

Twenty-five years later I was on a television program at the Truman Library with Averell Harriman, Clark Clifford, Matt Ridgeway and two or three others. It was the twenty-fifth anniversary of Korea. I said just what I said to you and I had my papers with me and Harriman got furious. He said, "The orders *were* clear." I said, "Well, let me read them aloud." There was a huge audience. I said, "Let me read them aloud." He said, "Don't pay attention to documents, pay attention to me, Luke." And I said, "Averell, that is not the way to write history." Those orders caused me some real heartache in many ways. But at any rate I thought they were ambiguous. It was one of the few times I really had a fight with Acheson. It was not the only time.

Important directions for American foreign policy were set in that particular era. There were a lot of very difficult times. We had not found our place in the world. We were struggling among ourselves. The McCarthy period was an appalling one with shocking results and a lot of incidents that were of major importance. I think the only good thing that came out of it is that I think people now identify McCarthyism when they see it and hear it and I hope will continue to do so. The statement that Dean Acheson made with respect to the Alger Hiss case weakened his whole period as secretary of state and weakened the administration. It was a very traumatic incident. I was deeply involved in it. It had quite a history actually.

John Foster Dulles was much closer to Alger than Dean was. Dean was close to his brother Donald Hiss but not to Alger; they really didn't know each other. But Dulles had been the great friend of Alger going back to the formation of the UN in California, San Francisco, and is the one who made him president of the Carnegie Endowment. When Alger got into all his trouble, Dulles, in effect, turned it around and ran the other way, probably wisely. And Acheson said, "I'm not going to do that. I'm not going to react that way," and after the first decision of the court he said to me, "I've got a press conference, what am I going to say about that?" I said, "Nothing." He said, "I'm not going to do that. That is what Dulles tried to do and I'm not going to do that. I have to stand on my relationships."

At any rate I wrote all night. I went to two other people who were at the time closest to Dean: Paul Nitze and Phillip Jessup; we were the three closest to Acheson. I said, "We've got to stop him, he's going to say something on this and he must not do it." So I wrote a little thing that said, "This is pending before the courts. It would be improper for me to comment." If he'd stayed with it, there would have been no problem. He said, "I think each of us who has a friend in trouble has to make his own decision with respect to what his relations will be with that individual." But he got in there and he got carried away. He added, "But I think you were trying to elicit more from me and I will not turn my back on Alger Hiss." That did it. It was a sensational incident and the mail that flowed in was unbelievable. Oddly enough it was overwhelmingly in Acheson's favor; but the press wasn't, the Congress wasn't, nothing else was, and it was a very unfortunate incident. It added fuel to the McCarthy kind of thing, of the pressures that were upon us, and I think did weaken the presidency.

There were other major achievements of the era, though, that I think we can look back on with great pride: the Marshall Plan; NATO, which has held up remarkably well; and our own posture in the world has crystallized. It will change, but at any rate we began to recognize, I think to a greater degree than we had before, what our posture was and what it should be. I think that President Truman—it rather surprised me how quickly this occurred—was looked back on as a great President. But at the time he left town nobody was sorry. He left and everyone was rather relieved: the public, the press.

Even then I felt it had been a very remarkable administration. The decisionmaking process was clear, there was not doubt about how things were going to run. The National Security Council had a staff of about three people and they didn't do anything, the Cabinet did it, and the National Security Council functioned in what seemed to me to be the way the NSC should function, and the secretary of state took the lead and the rest of the government in the field of foreign affairs participated within the limits of their own responsibilities as well as the Cabinet. But the President was constantly willing to delegate; he was constantly willing to stand behind his own decisions; he made no apologies for them; he seemed never to be troubled by them; he didn't wring his hands; he was eternally confident in what direction he wished to go and wished to take the nation. I think those are the qualities that in time made the administration stand out as so successful.

MR. THOMPSON: As usual, Luke Battle hasn't ducked the hard issues and he's giving you an opportunity to ask questions about some of the most contentious issues and some of the greatest achievements that took place in the Truman administration. Who'd like to ask the first question?

QUESTION: The Truman presidency established national and international policy that this country has followed since. Out of the Truman presidency came, as you say, a direction this country established.

MR. BATTLE: I don't want to take you into other presidencies, but I think it's terribly interesting to consider Vietnam and what were the roots of that problem—LBJ's conviction "I'm not going to be charged with the loss of China," which is what Truman was faced with. China wasn't ours to lose and if we had shut up about it things would have been better. Restraint is not one of our virtues. But the impact of that era and the contests between the right represented by Nixon, the charge of loss of China, all those things including the impact on us of Vietnam seem to me terribly important.

QUESTION: Suppose he were President at the time that JFK had to deal with the Castro situation. What do you think Truman would have done?

MR. BATTLE: It's awfully hard to answer that kind of question. You can make a case for direct intervention in Cuba, but you can't make any case for doing it the way we did.

QUESTION: But what would Truman have done?

MR. BATTLE: I don't know what he would have done. If he would have been caught between administrations, I have no idea. If he had faced it squarely, I suspect that he would have gone in.

QUESTION: I wonder if you look back to that period when Truman was President if you can think of any situations where you feel that an important opportunity was missed to change relationships with Russia or any initiative from them that perhaps might have been met with more generosity, more trust, more concern. Were there opportunities missed or was it a situation where there were no opportunities and a certain policy that was in place just kept on going?

MR. BATTLE: I've looked back on this question very seriously myself and I don't know. I think we got off in a direction, and we're on it now. We simply didn't explore carefully enough. There was no Kennan voice outside. We were oversimplistic as a nation seeing good only in the UN and righteousness only in the NATO direction. We had the atomic bomb in that early period, the Soviets didn't. There was a feeling I think of enormous righteousness on our part. I think we as a people are a little more sophisticated now in terms of looking at the world than we were then. I don't know of any major opportunity; there may have been one but I don't know of any.

QUESTION: Was the invitation to the Soviet Union and the Eastern European countries made in all sincerity?

MR. BATTLE: Let's just review what happened. I had an interesting conversation with Dean Acheson about this one time. I don't think anybody when the Marshall Plan started recognized what it was to become. I don't think anybody saw the scope that would develop. I don't think anyone recognized what we were moving into. I said to Acheson one day, "Did General Marshall really understand what he was saying?" He thought for a minute and said, "I think so." That's an interesting statement. Now if you remember Acheson floated the idea, as I mentioned earlier, in the Cleveland, Mississippi speech and got very little reaction; the Harvard speech got no reaction at all in Europe initially and very little in this country. Acheson got the foreign press together in Washington and said, "You fellows," about half a dozen, "you're missing the biggest opportunity you are ever going to have." And they rewrote the coverage on the Marshall speech. It got played in Europe and it got played back over here because it was suddenly a big story in Europe. But it took several days to build up. Everybody had a sense of direction and initially it included a belief that we had no choice but to try to make the Eastern Europeans participate. Whether anyone thought there was a chance of eastern participation was a strongly divisive issue. There were those who felt the Russians would probably come in and try to destroy and be disruptive. There were those who felt they would never do it. I am awfully glad we at least made an effort even though it may have been but halfhearted. I believe that senior people in our government at that point thought that we had to do it; if they accepted, we would have had to stand by our offer.

QUESTION: It passed by one vote, by the way.

QUESTION: We were speaking earlier about the continuities between the Eisenhower and Truman administrations. One thing that doesn't seem so continuous to me is Eisenhower's remarks upon the covert apparatus in the CIA. My understanding is that the people in the CIA in 1952 were in favor of intervening both in Iran and Guatemala and the Truman administration looked unfavorably on that. It wasn't until the Republicans came in that that was carried out. Do you think in retrospect Truman's attitude towards these covert operations was different than Eisenhower's and if so do you think he had the right attitude about this?

MR. BATTLE: I think that one of the tragedies of the whole history is that we let ourselves increasingly believe in covert activity. Now there is a place for covert activity but you don't need a covert action in every incident you have or every conflict you have in the world. We have overdone it in a large measure, and a lot of it is absolutely worthless. I've had a lot of experience with this and I assure you we let ourselves go overboard in the use of it. Now this is part of the maturing process of the United States as much as it was the intellectual differences between a Truman and an Eisenhower. I think it got to be more and more so and was at its height in the Nixon era. If you read some of the statements that have come out in recent days about if you don't like a world leader get rid of him, that's ridiculous. It evolved with a national sense of responsibility and involvement, and again the simplistic belief that if the world wasn't the way we wanted it we had to change it, we had to make it the way we wanted it. You can't do that. I think what happened in Iran is so long and complex a story I don't want to get into it here but the tragedy of Iran goes right straight through the fall of the Shah and involves the overuse and misuse in my judgment of two things: one was military sales and the other was covert intelligence.

MR. THOMPSON: From where you sat, was there the split that the documents seem to suggest on universalizing the Truman Doctrine between Acheson, Clifford, and Vandenberg who wanted the strongest possible statement of the worldwide threat, and people like Charles Bohlen, George Kennan and George Elsey who said we ought to make it a more discriminate statement?

MR. BATTLE: Well, there was a split on it, without any question. There was a feeling we ought to be a little more careful here. I never felt that Acheson wanted to make it universal—to some extent I have to say he was pushed along by the time. I think he became in his latter days much more militaristic and he and I reached the stage for the last two or three years, as much devoted as we had been to each other all these years, where there were many subjects and things we didn't deal with. But during the period of his secretaryship it seemed to me that he was remarkably balanced, remarkably restrained. There were serious arguments within from time to time for preemptive war. While we still had the superiority of the atomic bomb let's kill them. There was never any of that in Acheson's philosophy.

QUESTION: In the telegram that you referred to earlier, was MacArthur, historically speaking, guilty of insubordination?

MR. BATTLE: Yes, and not just on that count. It was not the Yalu that was insubordinate; it was his continuous statements to the Veterans of Foreign Wars and a whole series of other things and his enunciation of a policy that wasn't policy. He was told several times don't issue any more statements, no comments on this subject, and away he'd go. The march to the Yalu was consistent with his orders. I thought the orders were unfortunate, I said what I thought of it at the time. I was a staff officer in the Pacific during World War II. I had been on the receiving end of Mr. MacArthur's telegrams for a long period of time. I did not find him a particularly restrained man in any way, shape or form. I thought this was a very dangerous thing. And again there was an element of politics in the thing, I have to say. After the Inchon landing, nobody wanted to tell him, don't cross the 38th parallel or limit the move if you do, that was part of it. But you needed to put some restraint on how far he was supposed to go.

QUESTION: How did Dean Rusk stand on that particular issue?

MR. BATTLE: He was all for the telegram. He was standing beside me when I argued with Acheson.

MR. THOMPSON: One last question on politics. Was Truman a consummate politician?

MR. BATTLE: Don't misunderstand me, I don't consider Harry S. Truman without flaws. I think he had a lot of flaws. But in the main I think he did believe that he tried to do what was right, he really did.

When you got a head-on collision between right and politics, I think he might have a little trouble sometimes making up his mind. He was not a President without flaws, but he was remarkable in the context of history. Everyone was so delighted to see Carter leave town. You already are beginning to get a little bit of, "Well, Carter wasn't so bad. Why did we really mind Carter so much?" And Eisenhower has emerged as a much more positive figure than he appeared to be a few years ago. I think he looks a little bit better than I thought he would. Truman made a very quick comeback. In the mid-Eisenhower period, there was a poll of historians in the country and they gave Truman very high marks, and that was only a couple of years after he had been practically run out of town. It was a remarkable recovery for a man whom I didn't think would reemerge so quickly. I don't think Carter is going to be reborn that quickly, but it will be interesting to see.

MR. THOMPSON: I forgot to say that Luke Battle was with NATO in Paris and there are any number of other subjects that provide a good excuse for him to come back again and stay a little longer. We are delighted that you've come to talk with us about the Truman presidency.

MR. BATTLE: Thank you very much. It was a pleasure to be with you.

BIPARTISANSHIP
IN FOREIGN POLICY
Francis O. Wilcox

MR. THOMPSON: We are very pleased to have an opportunity to visit with Dean Francis Wilcox. In a previous interview on the Eisenhower presidency, Milton Eisenhower made the comment that the best thing he had done as President of Johns Hopkins was when he appointed Dean Wilcox as Dean of the School of Advanced International Studies. Today Dean Wilcox is the Director General of the Atlantic Council of the United States and has pioneered in a whole series of studies that have dealt with such vital issues as the future of NATO and the relationship between Congress and the President and foreign policy and other important questions.

We wondered, Fran, how you looked at the Truman presidency in history; how you saw the role that President Truman played in foreign policy; what you saw as the turning points in America's foreign relations in which he might have been a principle architect and how you assess the overall approach of the Truman presidency in foreign policy.

MR. WILCOX: I'm glad to comment briefly on some of these questions. My relationship with President Truman was not a close one in the sense that I was a part of his administration because I was working on Capitol Hill with the Senate Foreign Relations Committee during the time that he was President from 1945 at the time of the death of President Roosevelt until 1952 when President Eisenhower was elected.

Let me say at the outset that I not only have great admiration for Milton Eisenhower but I also feel great gratitude because I think what he did for me was certainly in the long run very helpful. I was grateful for that appointment, although the life of a dean is not a very easy one.

President Truman came into office at a very critical and important time in American history. I guess all periods are critical. At least they seem to have been since World War II. But this was at a time when the war was over and we were groping to find the most useful ways of constructing the bases for our foreign policy in the postwar period. That started, you will recall, with the approval of the United Nations Charter and our participation in all of the agencies of the United Nations that were created in the postwar period. In this regard, of course President Truman exercised a great deal of foresight in my judgment because while everybody wanted to join the United Nations we all had some reservations about our participation in it because we did not know quite what the Soviet Union would be doing. And those of us who went to the San Francisco conference were not entirely convinced that the United Nations would function satisfactorily. We recognized that it could do so only if the great powers were willing to participate in winning the peace as they had participated and worked together in winning the war.

After about three years, when the Soviet Union began to exercise its policies of expansionism—which they have been exercising with rather alarming frequency in more recent years—it became apparent that the United Nations was not going to function satisfactorily. So we moved in the direction of creating NATO, the alliance of the Western democracies. Just prior to that, of course, Britain had notified us that she would be pulling out of the Middle East because of her financial limitations and budgetary restrictions so President Truman came up with the Greek-Turkish aid program which preceded the NATO treaty in 1947. In that program he was able to win the support of a majority of the Senate and the House with a fairly sizeable majority. This was a remarkable achievement because aid to Greece and Turkey represented a very marked departure in our foreign policy. It marked, in effect, new paths and new directions because here we were saying that we would help those countries that were subjected to Communist pressures from the outside and Communist domination. And we served notice on the Soviet Union that they must not persist in their activities in Greece and Turkey. We also assured Greece and Turkey that we would be helpful to them in building the kind of economic and defense structures they needed in order to prevent Communist domination.

President Truman had an important vision here, a new departure. Some people thought it was as important as the Monroe Doctrine had been a hundred and twenty years before in charting new courses for American policy. Then came the NATO treaty which was again approved by a substantial majority in the Senate. That made quite clear—again a new departure—that the United States would come to the aid of any of our allies in the North Atlantic area who were attacked (presumably by the Soviet Union) and would be ready to help restore the peace and stability of the North Atlantic area. This again, was a very important and significant departure.

I should have mentioned, of course, in between the UN and the NATO Treaty, the Marshall Plan which was a very important development. Never had a great power expressed a willingness to extend aid on such a massive scale as was involved in the Marshall Plan, a sixteen billion dollar program for four years. The President, with the help of Senator Vandenburg and others, was able to win the support of a Republican controlled Senate at a time when these steps were tremendously important for the United States.

So I have always felt that he made a great contribution to our foreign policy. He had the capacity for making decisions that were daring and courageous. He always said that the buck stopped right at his desk and clearly he wasn't afraid to exercise that responsibility when the crises came. I feel that his role in the development of a nonpartisan foreign policy, and his role of leadership when he was able to carry the eightieth Republician Congress along with him was tremendously important. For these developments represented a real turning point in American history and a real turning point in our foreign policy. I would have to give him very high marks. I know that some of the polls in later years showed him rather low in public esteem but I think that as time goes by he will be recognized for what he was, a great President. And I think that his greatest contribution came in the form of the development of a bipartisan foreign policy at a very critical time in American history.

MR. THOMPSON: Do you think that he was able to bring about a bipartisan policy in part because he had friends and allies in the Congress, especially the Senate, but also Speaker Rayburn and others with whom he had warm, friendly personal relations? Was that an ingredient?

MR. WILCOX: I think it was. There is no question. When he left the Senate to take over the presidency he had a good many friends there. And he took his new post in an humble sort of way that won the admiration and the appreciation of his colleagues in the Senate and I think they were quite willing to support him whenever there was any question of doubt about their support. As a matter of fact I've found over the years that Congress treats their friends and colleagues very well—people who have worked there. They have a certain loyalty to the Hill and the Hill has a certain loyalty to them. And this was certainly true in the case of President Truman.

MR. THOMPSON: Did he have, when he was in the Senate, a close relation with Senator Vandenburg or did that come later through people like Robert Lovett and some of the rest of you?

MR. WILCOX: I think that came a little later. President Truman was a pretty strong Democrat and Senator Vandenburg was a pretty strong Republican and I don't think their ties were particularly close. Of course the Senate, as you know, is a big club and everybody is friendly with everybody else more or less. But I think the crucial period found Senator Vandenburg in a position of considerable responsibility which he took very seriously. He recognized that the Republican element in the Senate was not going to support the administration unless he took a strong role of leadership. So he worked with President Truman. He worked with Bob Lovett and George Marshall who were in the State Department at the time and they were obviously very helpful to the President in the evolution of this friendly relationship.

I think both Vandenburg and Truman saw the pressing need for the development of a bipartisan approach at a time when the world situation was really quite critical and it was important to move ahead to build a strong foreign policy for the postwar world.

MR. THOMPSON: Senator Vandenberg in the famous meeting that preceded the decision to go ahead with the Truman Doctrine, according to Dean Acheson and others, made it clear that unless the administration announced an overall global approach to meeting the challenge of world Communism that he didn't think the Congress would respond. Some others, George Kennan and George Elsey among them, and, it's a little hard to be sure but Charles Bohlen and George Marshall seemed to agree, would rather have had the issue formulated in terms of meeting Russian imperialism at specific places, not stated in the form of a global doctrine. But Senator Vandenberg, you will recall after Marshall's opening presentation, called on the administration to state its case more broadly and Dean Acheson did so in a very strong statement that attracted Vandenberg's attention. Do you think that part of the reason bipartisanship worked was that you had a very broad formulation of what the threat was and that if it had been anything less than that, simply a tactical statement of how you meet the next challenge whatever happened after Greece, that that kind of a statement would not have attracted bipartisan support?

MR. WILCOX: I think so. As you know, Senator Vandenberg was something of an isolationist before Pearl Harbor. But then he changed his approach; he recognized that the world was pretty interdependent and by the time the United Nations charter was created I think he went along pretty well with a more global approach towards things. This was expressed in a number of ways. When the Greek-Turkish program came along he was insistent that there be put into the legislation a clause which recognized the role of the United Nations in the settlement of differences and made it quite clear that if differences arose the United Nations decisions would be recognized.

And in the Marshall Plan he made it quite clear that this was an attempt to help develop our relations on a very wide basis. He departed from the idea of isolationism by 1963 when he made his famous speech about Germany. So he did have, I think, a statesmanlike approach towards world affairs which President Truman shared. The two leaders did see pretty much eye to eye on what we needed to do to contain the Communist threat at that time. This became more apparent by 1948 when Russia and the Eastern European bloc decided not to join the Marshall Plan, for example, and when the Soviet Union began to cast more and more vetoes in the Security Council of the United Nations.

MR. THOMPSON: Your colleague, Paul Nitze, has said on a couple of occasions that when you testify in Congress you better be sure you make your case the strongest one you can for the policy you seek support for and that is one of the reasons that some of the early policies in the Cold War might have been stated in the very most extreme form. Is that generally true when you send a person to testify before a congressional committee or is it more like a seminar at Johns Hopkins?

MR. WILCOX: Well, I think it is true. You do have to persuade those who are about to pronounce upon the program—those who are going to approve a bit of legislation or an appropriation bill that you want approved. You do have to persuade them that you have a good case. The work that we went through, for instance, to get the Marshall Plan ready, the documents that we compiled and the testimony that we had, the witnesses from every quarter—this was a good case in point. Certainly the administration tends to overemphasize, to exaggerate a bit, and the effect of all the testimony and the witnesses and the commissions that were set up during the Marshall Plan period did tend to overwhelm the opposition. It is perhaps a trait of the executive branch that in order to make their case persuasively before a group of skeptical congressmen, they have to exaggerate a bit and underline the important things they feel can be accomplished. If they were to present all of the weaknesses and the dubious points about a particular program, Congress would certainly tend to react in a negative fashion. It's only natural that those who are making the case should make it as strongly as the situation will permit.

MR. THOMPSON: Do you think that there is anything to the theory that the Truman/Acheson policy, because it had to be stated very strongly, and because there was emphasis on recreating a balance of power through building situations of strength, tended to downgrade a little bit the type of thing Churchill was calling for, negotiations with the Soviets at the summit? You recall that even in the Fulton speech, which was always looked on as a scare speech by liberals in this country, Churchill said that we ought to be prepared to meet the Russians at the highest level to negotiate. But it is often said that Truman and Acheson did not leave that possibility open. Is that a fair or is that an unfair comment, do you think?

MR. WILCOX: That is a difficult question. I do remember in the hearings of the Senate Foreign Relations Committee when Dean Acheson was being considered for the post of secretary of state, Senator Vandenberg wrote out for him a statement which he was willing to make about his attitude toward Communism because some people thought that Dean Acheson was a little soft on Communism. This would suggest that as secretary of state he didn't do anything that would discourage discussions with the Soviet Union but he made it quite clear in his statement that he was strongly opposed to Communism and therefore the committee approved him, as I recall, unanimously. But if he hadn't done that there was some question as to whether he had a strong enough conviction about Communism to justify being secretary of state.

MR. THOMPSON: One last question in this vein. Averell Harriman has said that when he came back from Moscow and met with the new President, President Truman, he felt he had to warn him and he hoped that he would stiffen his spine or words to that effect. So Harriman warned him. But he said he didn't mean that Truman should talk as strongly to Molotov in their famous meeting as he did. Is there anything to the proposition that Truman took the advice of people who knew what the Soviet Union was up to and then reacted even more strongly than they would have reacted or is that an after the fact comment that isn't valid?

MR. WILCOX: I don't know if I can shed any light on that question. I know all Presidents get their information from a variety of sources and it depends on the President and the source as to which information is most influential in guiding the President in his decisions. But as I recall now the discussions we had in the Foreign Relations Committee of the Senate, the news that was coming in from all over the world was not very encouraging—particularly the unfavorable developments in the Middle East and the withdrawal of the British from that area, and the difficulties that were arising in Greece, Turkey and Yugoslavia, the continued maintenance under arms of four million or more Soviet troops and the reduction of troops in the United States and western Europe, the failure of the United Nations to keep the peace as we had hoped it might be able to do, etc. These things added up to the point where I think Mr. Truman felt he had to take a fairly tough line against the Soviet Union.

MR. THOMPSON: As I remember, you were Assistant Secretary for International Organization Affairs and always had a strong view about the constructive function that the United Nations at its best could play. Did President Truman give sufficient support to the United Nations?

MR. WILCOX: I think so. He had not been close to UN developments in 1943 and 1944, not nearly as close as President Roosevelt had been, so that when Mr. Roosevelt died and President Truman took over he was confronted with a whole host of problems at that point in the postwar period. It was only natural that he would be somewhat less enthusiastic about the United Nations. But he gave it his full support. He appointed a strong delegation that went to San Francisco. I couldn't quarrel at all with his decisions about that. He gave it his full support and I'm sure he hoped it would work. But then we all became convinced later on in the 1940s—1948, 1949—that the basic principle of the United Nations, which called for the continued cooperation of the great powers, was not going to work in practice and we would have to do the best we could with an organization that just did not live up to our expectations.

MR. THOMPSON: You've lived in at least three worlds, the Congress as chief of staff of the Senate Foreign Relations Committee; the executive branch in the Department of State; and you could have had a variety of ambassadorships. Then you moved to the third area, the deanship of a major school of international affairs at one of our great universities. You must have viewed from the three different perspectives a number of Presidents. How would you compare President Truman in terms of his grasp of world affairs, his style of leadership, his use of staff and people, and those who surrounded him? Every President is often both praised for some of the people who surround him and also criticized for some of them. In all these areas how would you compare President Truman with other Presidents you've known?

MR. WILCOX: That's a tough question to throw at anybody. I did not know President Truman as well as I knew President Eisenhower. I worked closely with President Johnson when he was on Capitol Hill and I knew President Ford and President Nixon better than I knew President Truman. I would have to rank President Truman quite high despite that fact that he showed up poorly in the polls in the latter part of his term. I'd have to rate him quite high with the others in terms of his grasp of the subject matter. He wasn't brought into the presidency as one who had a great knowledge of world affairs. He hadn't had as much training or experience as the others. He'd been chairman of the special committee on war problems, I've forgotten the exact title of that committee but it was very influential during the war. Some people, I think, didn't expect him to do too well as President but he was a great reader of history. I was impressed by his interest in historical developments in various parts of the world over the centuries. He seemed to have a capacity for making tough decisions and this is what the presidency is all about. I used to tell my classes, when they complained about the President and the fact that he made a decision they did not like: "Well, the President never gets questions to decide upon unless they are really tough questions. All of the easy questions are settled somewhere below him. If the President were to get credit for all the easy questions that he might decide upon, his score card would look much better. But the fact is that he only gets the really tough problems and he's bound to make some mistakes—at least in the eyes of certain people."

President Truman had the capacity to use his staff well. He selected people with capacity and ability and that of course is a great plus in terms of Presidents. When you look at the mistakes other Presidents have made in bringing into the inner circle of the White House a good many people from their own states who may not have had much ex-

perience in the field of foreign policy, you begin to realize how important this quality is. Mr. Carter did that when he brought in nine people
from Georgia and put them around him in the White House. Mr.
Reagan did the same thing when he brought in several people as his
principal advisers who have had no background or experience in
foreign policy. I think Mr. Truman used very good judgment in the
selection and placement of his people and he utilized their abilities very
well. I could go on and compare him with Mr. Johnson and Mr. Ford
and the others but I think I won't try to do that.

But I do think he really deserves a great deal of credit. He didn't
want the presidency. He took it rather reluctantly and in the circumstances this is understandable. But then he took hold and did a
corking good job in my judgment and I'm talking mainly about
foreign policy problems. He was faced with so many tough decisions,
and so many places where new departures had to be made, where new
concepts had to be analyzed and approved. He handled them very
effectively.

MR. THOMPSON: If he were President today do you think he could
make bipartisanship work given what changes have occurred?

MR. WILCOX: Maybe not. The fact is, as you well know, that after
the war there was a consensus in this country that revolved around the
feeling that we had won a great war, a great sacrifice had been made,
and we had to prepare for the peace. We were united in our stand
against Nazi aggression and we were united in our determination to
take those steps that would help make the world a more peaceful and
more stable place to live in. There was a sizeable consensus in this
country, developed to a great extent by Arthur Vandenberg whose role
in shaping Republican support and whose role in history I think has
not been quite appreciated by the people of the United States. There
were very special reasons why bipartisanship or nonpartisanship
evolved so successfully in that period. Now of course that unity, that
consensus, has disappeared partly because of Vietman and partly
because of other circumstances. Whether a Mr. Truman and a Mr.
Vandenburg could now evolve out of the present order of things a real
consensus on foreign policy, I don't know. That consensus was certainly not shown in the Panama Canal case nor has it been shown in
the arms control area where the SALT Treaty was negotiated by several Presidents and then not approved by the Senate. There are a good
many other examples of our failure to secure a nonpartisan vote on important foreign policy issues such as the AWAC sales, the Turkish
arms embargo, the Rhodesian chrome problem, etc. The consensus

has fallen away and it is one thing that we need to work on today—the development of a new consensus. And to do it you need a willingness on the part of the White House and on the part of the leaders in Congress to work together for the common good.

MR. THOMPSON: Your good friend and ours Dean Rusk often says that President Truman had an ability to look at a group of straws that made up all the intricate and complex issues, and then pull out one that was the most crucial straw and simplify both the formulation and explanation of policy in terms of that central issue, for example, resistance to Communism, or the reconstruction and rebuilding of Europe or the United Nations. Is it that our issues and problems have become so much more complex that simplification is impossible today or is it that we haven't had anybody who in recent times had that peculiar knack and who was convincing and credible in the way that he simplified complex issues?

MR. WILCOX: I think it is true that the issues have become much more complex in recent years. If you go back to the middle of the nineteenth century a President might have on his desk two or three important issues during the year in the field of foreign policy, and now he has a dozen or fifteen or twenty that will come up. Some are more critical than others but certainly the issues have become more complex and I have the greatest sympathy for the man who sits in the White House and has to make the final decisions.

I must say again though that these things can be worked out if you have the kind of leadership in the White House and on Capitol Hill which responds to responsibility and the need for cooperation between the two branches. We spoke a moment ago of the sizeable vote that Mr. Truman got on the Greek-Turkish program. Well, one reason he got that vote stemmed from the fact that Senator Vandenburg and I sat down for a good many hours working out questions that the Senate members might wish to ask about that program. The Senator knew that there were a number of Republicans who would not go along with the program unless they were completely satisfied that the answers to all their questions were available. We compiled a sizeable list of questions and we got answers from the Department of State for each one—I think there were, as I recall, about a hundred of them. We printed the document and circulated it to all members of the Senate. We invited them to the hearings. The Senator was very careful on the floor of the Senate, so solicitous that he answered in considerable detail every question that was put to him by his colleagues—and there were a good many. As he put it "we will kill the enemy with kindness."

So he was able to carry the Senate members of the Republican party along with him and to assure Mr. Truman the kind of majority that he needed to get the Greek-Turkish program underway.

Things like that were done during this period perhaps more than they are now partly because of the consensus in the country and partly because of the attitude of mind and the leadership that President Truman and Senator Vandenburg demonstrated.

MR. THOMPSON: You did say that "Senator Vandenburg and I sat down." When I was in graduate school there was a group of you who were always mentioned as people that were respected in the public service and civil service—Andy Goodpaster in the military would be another example. Surely President Truman didn't speak of the career service or the leaders in high positions in either the legislative or executive branch as people that were merely spending taxpayer's money. Do you think the disparagement of the public service has made bipartisanship and cooperation more difficult today or has it always been the practice to downplay the people who played staff role and were key in either the executive or legislative branch?

MR. WILCOX: Well, I don't want to downplay the role of the staff members on Capitol Hill. They are certainly very important. Indeed you hear a good deal of criticism now to the effect that they are playing too important a role. There are too many of them, it is argued, and they get their bosses to do all kinds of things that they wouldn't be inclined to do if they weren't encouraged by their staff. Staff members write speeches for the senators, they prepare resolutions for them to introduce, and they get into all kinds of complications that they wouldn't get into if they didn't have that much staff help. The staff has to earn their money after all.

MR. THOMPSON: You do hear things that I don't ever remember hearing about some of you who played a role earlier—namely, that they are a highly upward mobile group, that they are quick learners, that they move from one thing to another. You and Pat Holt and Carl Marcy and a number of others stuck with jobs for a considerable period of time and the academic community by and large and the journalistic community had good things to say about the service that you rendered. I've wondered whether you were part of the cement that held the thing together a little bit more than the current group holds it together.

MR. WILCOX: Well, this is again a complicated problem. In the earlier days when we had a consensus in the field of foreign policy, and when the Foreign Relations Committee was dominated by a kind of spirit of nonpartisanship, the staff was appointed not on the basis of politics but on the basis of the capacity to do the job. The professional staff was set up that way.

I stayed on as chief of staff under four different chairmen, two Republicans and two Democrats and I always insisted that the staff be able and willing to serve both sides of the aisle whether they were Republican or Democratic. This philosophy worked reasonably well during that period. More recently, however, there was a demand from the minority group that they be given staff members of their own, assigned to the minority members. This broke down any semblance of nonpartisanship in the staff so that there has been more recently a more rapid turnover of staff directors on Capitol Hill with new congressmen coming in, new chairmen coming in, and appointing new staff directors and new staff members. This is understandable in the field of labor and other domestic problems but I'm disappointed that it has worked out that way in the field of foreign relations. I'd rather see the staff nonpartisan in character and able and willing to serve both Republicans and Democrats. This would certainly help the Congress approach foreign policy problems in a nonpartisan manner.

And so many of our foreign policy problems do cut across party lines. Even with respect to the Panama Canal Treaty, President Carter said without the support of the Republicans he wouldn't have gotten that through the Senate. Howard Baker was very instrumental in getting it approved. Where you have the treaty process involved you always need two-thirds of the Senate to support the administration. Consequently, you have to have a nonpartisan or a bipartisan approach. Nothing else will work.

MR. THOMPSON: Do you think there is anything that can be done about this or do you think that the project on which the Atlantic Council and The Former Members of Congress are embarking on can throw some light on this?

MR. WILCOX: The project you refer to has to do with the changing relationship between Congress and the executive branch in foreign policy. I think we can throw a good deal of light on it. The question remains as to how the light will be reflected and what people in positions of influence do about it. You and I could work out a good many reasonable suggestions but when politics is involved, when party issues come to the fore, when people are concerned about getting control of the White House or getting control of the Senate or the House, sometimes these basic principles are lost in the scramble. The big question is to get people to accept the good ideas after you have formulated them. I think it was Frederick the Great who was given the famous peace plan of the Abbey de St. Pierre. His aide sat with him while he read it and he said, "Sire, what do you think of the proposal?" Frederick the Great is reported to have said, "Well, it is a remarkable plan. It is precise in every detail. All we need now is the consent of Europe and a few similar trifles."

And I think that is true with many of these major issues. You can set up presidential commissions, you can set up study groups. You can embark upon projects that are designed to get at basic truths and recommendations. But the question remains whether they will be accepted by those in positions of power and responsibility. Some of the Senate leaders know what needs to be done on Capitol Hill to improve the Senate and the House to make them more effective in the legislative process and the foreign policy process, but they have trouble getting the approval of their colleagues for necessary changes. Many of them don't want to divest themselves of little things they do that make their lives very burdensome. They continue to do relatively unimportant things on Capitol Hill which they don't need to do any longer and then they complain that their work schedule is too heavy. It does not make sense.

When the Congressional Reorganization Act of 1945 was passed, sixteen Senate committees were created—standing committees of the Senate—and it was assumed that the work of the Senate could be done by these standing committees. But what has happened? Well, everybody wants to be a committee chairman, to have the prerequisites of a chairman on Capitol Hill. So they proceed to set up a whole raft of subcommittees so many members of the majority party can become a chairman of a subcommittee. This defies the basic principles which underlay the Reorganization Act of 1945 but it also reflects political realities.

MR. THOMPSON: We are most grateful to you for giving us this time and we do agree with you that President Truman's leadership in the bipartisan foreign policy area was one of his greatest contributions. It has been very helpful to have someone who has seen it from several different angles to comment on it.

MR. WILCOX: Thank you, Ken. I do think that when the history of this period is recorded that this will be listed as his greatest achievement—the development of a bipartisan foreign policy at a very critical time in our history that enabled our country to meet effectively the great challenges of the postwar period. I think this will be considered his greatest contribution.

IV
TRUMAN:
AN
APPRAISAL

TRUMAN AND NATIONAL SECURITY
Frank Pace

MR. THOMPSON: Frank Pace needs no introduction in a group like this. He has established his credentials in three areas: first in government as secretary of the Army, director of the Bureau of the Budget, and in a host of other positions, at least some of which were in the period about which we hope to talk this afternoon; secondly, in the field of business at the highest level, for example at General Dynamics and finally in that very important area that deTocqueville wrote about in an early point in our history, of citizens who see the business of the republic of as much importance as any other business they may be engaged in. In my last years at the Rockefeller Foundation, one of the things that impressed us most was what Frank Pace did with the effort to send retired business and educational leaders into the developing countries, some 9,000 of them under the auspices of the International Executive Services who went with the highest professional credentials to help areas of need in the developing countries. In the absence of trained manpower, whether in the university, the government, or the business sphere, there was little if anything other foreign assistance agencies could do. Frank Pace tried to fill that void.

Today we continue our series on Portraits of American Presidents focusing on the Truman presidency, and nobody is better qualified and better positioned in history to talk with us about the Truman presidency than Frank Pace.

MR. PACE: Thank you. I'd better put myself in perspective with my audience by pointing out to you that when I graduated from the Harvard Law School and prepared to return to my native Little Rock, Arkansas, I had a very difficult task in front of me. My father was one of the South's most distinguished trial lawyers and he had expected me to join his law firm. I said to him, "Father, I'm not going to join your law firm." "Why not, son?" I said, "Sir, for two reasons." He said, "What are they?" I said, "One is I haven't earned it and two, you'd dominate me." "You're wrong on both counts." "I thought you'd feel that way, sir, but I'm not going to join your law firm." "What would you like to do?" "I'd like to become an assistant district attorney." "What, a son of mine work for the government?" I said, "Yes, sir." He said, "Well, I'll help you then." The assistant district attorney encompassed three counties in the state of Arkansas and the legislature, in its infinite wisdom, had voted the position but had established no salary appropriation. My distinguished father loved to say that in his judgment it was the only time I was ever rewarded for my service with the government. So much for my past.

I went on from that position to become general counselor of the Revenue Department, and after the war I went into the Department of Justice as an assistant attorney general in the taxation division. I was happily engaged in that when Bob Hannigan, who was postmaster general and also head of the Democratic National Committee, said to Tom Clark, the attorney general, "This is too much for me to handle. I have to have somebody to run the post office." So Tom Clark said, "I think I have a young man named Frank Pace who can do the job," and so I went over to meet with Bob Hannigan and I agreed to stay and run the post office. When Mr. Hannigan left he had said to the President that he felt that I was qualified to do other things. About that time Jim Webb, who was director of the budget, asked me if I wanted to become the deputy director of the budget. I had not known Jim except very casually. I don't know where he came to the conclusion I could do that horrendous job but somehow he did.

A few days later the President, Mr. Truman, asked me to come over. I had met him casually and he referred to Bob Hannigan and he said, "I think you have more to do in the government and I would like to offer you the position of chairman of the Civil Aereonautics Board.

The CAB was very glamorous back in those days. The world routes were being set up for TWA and Pan Am, and it was one of the exciting positions. I said, "Mr. President, I don't want you to think that I'm not very grateful but I'd like to give this some thought. If I may I'll be back tomorrow." And I did come back the next day and I said, "Mr. President, don't think I'm not grateful for the opportunity but I think I can serve you better as deputy director of the budget." Well, in his usual superb way he said, "Well, Frank, this is what I hoped you would do but I didn't think you would." So he made everything easy for me, which he did all the way through. He came from Missouri and I came from Arkansas and that gave us a little commonality that moved us ahead very well over the years.

I worked there under Jim Webb as deputy director for a year and a half. Webb was a magnificent man. He treated me as though I were a younger brother. Everybody took me under his wing and sought to complete my education, and I'll tell you the mastery of the Bureau of the Budget is one great big education. That's no country boy opportunity. I learned and enjoyed it tremendously, and in that process came to know Mr. Truman quite well. I'll give you a couple of incidents when I became director of the budget, which I did immediately after his election and Jim became under secretary of state, but two incidents are worth going over because they are revealing.

First, there was a project called the Central Arizona Project, which was a project to separate the waters of the Colorado and share them between Arizona and southern California. They'd gone in the past to southern California, and Arizona wanted its share. Truman did a very wise thing: he never politicized what came to the Bureau of the Budget. It never came in a politicized form, it came in a perfectly clean form. Any politicization of it could only come after we had made the decision based totally on the facts. I don't think that's been followed as effectively as it might over the years.

I went over this project. It was far too expensive to justify, and I said to the President, "I regret to say, Mr. President, this is far too expensive to justify, but I know Senator Hayden is your oldest friend in the Senate and Senator McFarland has voted with you on every issue."
"Well," he said, "Frank, is it close?" and I said, "No, sir." He said, "Is it clearly excessive?" I said, "Yes, sir." I saw a frown pass cross his face and he said, "Will you meet with Senators Hayden and McFarland and myself this afternoon?" I said, "Yes, sir." I came in and they were chatting in the Oval Office and he said, "Frank, tell Carl and Mac what you told me," and I got about half way through and Senator Hayden could see where it was going and he said, "Harry,

you can't do this to us." That was the only time in my entire period with Mr. Truman that I ever heard him referred to in the Oval Office or anywhere else other than Mr. President except by Mrs. Truman. And the President overlooked it because of Senator Hayden and said, "This will be totally destructive to Carl and myself and it's just not something you can afford to do." "Well," he said, "Carl, you heard what Frank said." He said, "Yes, I heard that but this is compelling." He said, "I'm sorry, Carl, I'll have to follow Frank's recommendation." Senator Hayden never spoke to him again, and McFarland was defeated at the next election, and I knew that he was a great man.

This was the day when the little haberdasher, the Pendergast man, went way up in my estimation and I knew differently. History is now vindicating that view.

The second incident shows very special Trumanesque qualities. The Marshall Plan had been adopted by the Congress and signed by the President. He called me and said, "Frank, for the Marshall Plan to succeed it needs a great salesman. And the greatest salesman in this country is Paul Hoffman, and he is going to be in my office this afternoon. I want to try to persuade him to undertake this assignment and I'd like you to be there because there may be some details to discuss about how this will work out." I said, "It will be a privilege, sir" and I was there. The President was, one-on-one, a great salesman, and the Marshall Plan was a hell of a sales object. But it was clear that Paul wasn't buying. He said, "Mr. President, I served in World War II. My company, the Studebaker Company, is in dreadful condition. I've agreed to stay there no less than three years as chairman. I've told my wife I will not come back to public service." The President could see how it was going. He said, "Now Paul, you don't want to make a hasty decision. I want you to go home, talk about this over the weekend with your wife and then come back and give me your decision on Monday." And then with that familiar Truman twinkle, he said, "Frank, stay a moment." Paul went on and he said, "Frank, I'm a kindly man. This is going to be a very dreadful weekend for Paul. His wife is going to upbraid him and he's going to struggle with his conscience. In the end he'll decide to do it." He said, "I'm going to save him all that pain. I'm going to announce he's accepted." He called in Charlie Ross and he announced it to the press. When Paul Hoffman got home that night, he said, "Dear," and she said, "Don't dear me!" He said, "What's wrong?" She said, "You accepted." He said, "What?" The President said, "Obviously, Frank, you're going to have to be here Monday when we talk together about that."

So great was the power of the Oval Office that Paul Hoffman never mentioned the fact that the President had preempted his decision, he never once mentioned it. And we got to discussing how this would work. The President got a little bored and he said, "Frank, why don't you and Paul go in the Cabinet Room and figure out how this thing will work—the fate of Europe, $30 billion, no charts, no staff, go figure out how this thing will work." So we went in to figure out how it would work and Paul made me promise that I would never tell what he said he could do it for, because he said we'd need ten times that to get it done.

But that was one of Truman's great strengths: he was capable of saying very complicated things in a very simple way without cheating. All the great mountebanks of history, McCarthy, Wallace, the greatest of them all Huey Long, have said very complicated things in a very simple way but they all cheated. And Mr. Truman had that rare talent. He had the ability to say things so the ordinary man and woman really understands. The world has gotten so hideously complicated. It's gotten so unbelievably complicated that most ordinary citizens don't understand. How long has it been since anybody in this room has heard somebody say, "My country, my U.S.A." Think about it. Have you heard that? I heard it a lot when I grew up. When I was growing up in the South, "My country" came out pretty regularly. That's not a reflection on our people, it's just a reflection of the fact that it's gotten to be too big to be "My country." And we've got to stop that because the system won't work if you don't feel like it's your country. He had that talent to a great degree. He had obviously great courage. "The buck stops here" was on his desk and it did stop there. He never backed away from it.

Then there was another thing. He had an overweening pride and love of the Oval Office. At least twice he said to me, "Frank, as Harry Truman I'm not very much, but as President Truman I have no peer." Those are big words. That enabled him to deal with the likes of George Catlett Marshall, Dean Acheson, Clark Clifford, all of whom were his intellectual superiors, without any concern. If Mr. Carter had had that same capacity we might have seen a different world. But Mr. Truman was President. And the things that hurt me in the years since Mr. Truman has been in some instances the casual and in other instances the highly improper fashion in which the Oval Office has been used by its occupants. That sense of glory in the presidency, that sense of glory in the Oval Office is a very essential part of this society and he had it in spades.

I left the budget to become secretary of the Army. Six weeks after I went there the Korean War broke out. My wife and I were at Joe Alsop's at dinner and Dean Rusk got a call from Dean Acheson that North Korea had invaded and he came over and told me. I said good night to Peg and told her that I would not be home that night and went to the Pentagon where I spent the night. Peg tells me that at their table they speculated why we had to leave and Joe Alsop identified Korea which was at that time almost unknown to any American. It was a faraway, distant, not strategically important place that suddenly broke out into a major requirement. It did and within a month, six weeks, it brought on the man who impacted most on my life, General George Catlett Marshall, who is of all the glorious human beings I've known the most glorious. He was one of the reasons why Mr. Truman was so successful.

There was no one who commanded Mr. Truman's respect and esteem like George Catlett Marshall. He had a very remarkable capacity. I never saw him face a major issue but what he placed that issue in a long-term perspective. That is one of the great problems of our society, and we find it in every facet of life. The quarterly report in the business world is a time bomb that means you can't think beyond three months because you've got to show an advance between the last quarter and this quarter. It may be an even shorter term than that in our national government. Our capacity really to think beyond today gets to be almost nonexistent. And if I could have a wish for Mr. Reagan it would be that George Catlett Marshall could come back and sit at his right hand because the decisions that are made there and the decisions that have been made over a large number of presidencies are decisions that may have some immediate values but have long-range dangers for the society.

I remember when General Marshall sent me to the first NATO meeting to represent him. He was chairman of the defense ministry. And to show how the world has changed, I remember when I was flying back I took my chief of staff "Lightning Joe" Collins and that brilliant staff man, General Al Grunther. In going back we flew over the Pyrenees to outline how you could protect Europe if and when the Russians overran all of Europe. Now I doubt anybody's memory goes back to the fact that that was a very realistic possibility in those years when I was there in 1950—had they chosen to do it, there was no doubt that that they could do it.

But General Marshall sent me to three other NATO meetings to represent him and he also sent me to Wake Island. I remember coming back from Wake Island. General Bradley was there with Admiral Radford, and reporting to General Marshall. And I said, "General Marshall, General MacArthur has stated that the war will be over by Thanksgiving and the boys home by Christmas." And he said, "Pace, that troubles me." I said, "You must not have heard me, General Marshall, General MacArthur says the war will be over by Thanksgiving, the boys home by Christmas." He said, "I heard you, Pace, and it has major short-range advantages for us, but long-range it has some problems because we've always felt that the function of war was to win or lose, like a football game. And since we've won, that's a very happy determination. But from now on wars can only be fought in pursuance of the necessary security of this society and very often will not be won or lost. I am afraid that that fact has not come home fully to the American people." I said, "But General Marshall, a great deal of water has gone under the dam since World War II. Would you say I was naive if I said the American people had learned their lesson?" He looked at me with those cold, blue eyes, and brother, they were cold, and he said, "No, Pace, I wouldn't say you were naive. I'd say you were *incredibly* naive." Then a slow smile crossed that Olympian countenance and I knew I'd been had. For that I had no comeback. But for some reason or other he put his trust in me. I went with Dean Acheson to four of the NATO meetings. I came to know that remarkable man.

Later, it started out just as an incidence of that remark of General MacArthur, but it was a very interesting thing to see develop. I came back to the Army General staff and said, "This is what General MacArthur has said. I don't want to come up next January to a congressional committee and have them say, 'Did General MacArthur say that the war would be over by Thanksgiving, that the boys would be home by Christmas?' 'Yes, sir.' 'What did you do?' 'Nothing.' I can't say that." I said, "What, in your judgment, is the easiest thing to select for reducing?" and they said, "Ammunition." I said, "Well, what can you cut it by?" and they said, "You can cut it by a third." I said, "Cut it by a fourth." Well, the war was *not* over by Thanksgiving, the boys were *not* home by Christmas, and I had lead time burned into my soul because I could not get that ammunition back up. General Van Fleet who succeeded General Ridgeway acted like every day was the fourth of July. He shot more ammunition than we were shooting in World War II and I was bleeding to get those bullets back in place and never did.

After the election I was exhausted. I've kept myself in good physical condition all my life. It was the only time I have ever been totally exhausted. I went off for a time and when I came back, Stu Symington called me and said, "Joe McCarthy has asked for a hearing of the Armed Services Committee in which he intends to lay the loss of life in Korea on your failure to provide adequate ammunition." I said, "Well, Stu, my staff is scattered and my records are difficult to follow," and he said, "That's a matter purely of academic interest, Frank. I just want you to know that's what's going to happen. It's up to you to figure out what to do about it." Well, by good fortune, I had been a very close friend of Senator Harry Byrd, Senior. I'd been down to his lovely estate with the apple orchards. When I was director of the budget he had been the reason why I balanced the budget twice. So I went to him and told him the story. He said, "Frank, I wouldn't worry." I said, "Why, thank you very much, senator, I don't think I'm going to pass a very pleasant night but I'm glad you don't want me to worry." So I arrived the next day and klieg lights were there. McCarthy had never touched me all during this period when he was belaboring the Truman administration, he never touched me even once.

I had an interesting device, by the way. For the first time I appointed a civilian general counsel of the Army. If there's anything that's sacred in the Army it's the judge advocate general, and that was not a very popular move. I set out a prescription that anything that the Army did wrong, I wanted it understood that if it was reported immediately, unless it were in violation of specific laws, I would overlook it. I had it brought to my civilian general counsel. I knew that the Congress was never interested in investigating anything it didn't discover itself. So I'd have my general counsel go up and say the secretary has discovered this, he'd like to know would you investigate it or would you like him to investigate it? They would say, "Let the secretary investigate it." So I escaped the slings and arrows of outrageous fortune, but apparently they had all come on me at once.

So I got there, McCarthy was there, the klieg lights were there, and Senator Byrd said, "Mr. Secretary, we're here to investigate the loss of life due to lack of ammunition and it's troublesome to us." I said, "Well, Mr. Chairman, not as troublesome as it is to me. I have a great concern." I then related how this had happened with General MacArthur. He said "Well, as I understand it, Mr. Secretary, you did this on the advice of General MacArthur," and I said, "Yes, sir." He said, "That was General Douglas B. MacArthur, was it not?" I said, "Yes, sir," and the klieg lights never turned on and I wasn't asked another question. I was saved by a Virginian, which is maybe one reason why I'm here.

It was a very interesting period. I saw much less of the President in this period than I had previously. I went over on one or two occasions when he suggested it, none when I did. The one thing I had done when

I had taken the assignment was to say that any directions I got from the White House I'd prefer to have them directly from him and not from General Vaughan, and that troubled him a little and he said, "Why do you say that?" I said, "Because I know when I hear it from you it's what you want, and when I hear it from General Vaughan it may or may not be." "Well," he said, "Frank, I'm not so sure of that." "Well," I said, "I'm not sure either, I'm just asking your indulgence." So anything he wanted me to do he either conveyed it through General Marshall or directly.

In this whole period the buildup of difficulty between General MacArthur, the Joint Chiefs, and the President was growing. General MacArthur sent the letter to the Veterans of Foreign Wars and also to Speaker Joe Martin, neither of which I believe a senior commander would normally have sent. I was on a routine inspection trip in the Far East and when I arrived I had the intercom on in my plane and I got down through the smog and fog that was always there in Tokyo to about 400 feet and it said, "Rise and circle the field—General MacArthur has not arrived." I said to my pilot, "The hell we'll rise and circle the field. You'll land and we'll wait for General MacArthur." Well, we landed and he was there and we trooped the line together. I always wondered whether he'd seat me on his right because by protocol I was entitled to that but I had to remember when he was Chief of Staff of the U.S. Army, I was a senior at Little Rock High School. But as you might imagine he was true to his colors and he seated me on his right. I stayed at his quarters; he gave a dinner in my honor. I received a cable from General Marshall saying, "This is explicit. Keep this as explicit. You will proceed to Korea where you will stay until you hear from me," and it didn't say a day, a week, a month, a year. And I had had some part in the assignment of General Ridgeway of whom I was very fond, who incidentally was probably one of the great field commanders that the world ever knew. I saw Korea under General Walker and three months later I saw it under General Ridgeway and it was a different world, a totally different world—there was pride, there was bearing. If you talk about leadership, I want you to know that that man had it in spades. He had all that Patton had plus something up here. Anyway, we went around and did all the things that you do normally. We decorated soldiers on the field. We also did something you shouldn't do—we flew in a light plane over the Chinese lines. About ten minutes after we landed there was a hail storm; if it had come ten minutes sooner we'd have been the first two captured by the Chinese.

I went to the headquarters of General John Throckmorton who was a friend of mine. There was a call there from Seoul. General Lev Allen said, "I have a cablegram for you from General Marshall." I said, "Read it to me," and it read as follows: "Disregard my cable number 8503. You will advise General Matthew B. Ridgeway that he is now the commanding general of the South Pacific. Vice General MacArthur relieved. You will proceed to Tokyo where you will participate with General Ridgeway in assuming the instance of his command." I said, "Read that once more, Lev." So he read it once more. I got General Ridgeway. You know he had those live grenades he carried. I said, "Get those live grenades off. If a hail storm hits one of them we're not going to get very far." He took them off and I took him out and the hail was beating down on the helmet. "General Ridgeway," I said, "it's my duty to inform you you're now the commanding general of the South Pacific. Vice General MacArthur is relieved." He said, "I can't believe it, Mr. Secretary." I said, "I can't either, so I'll repeat it. South Pacific Vice General MacArthur relieved." I said, "Now Matt, I'm to participate with you in assuming the instance of your command and I suggest we need to give General MacArthur twenty-four hours to arrange his affairs. So we'll wait here and let's go find out about that cablegram number 8503."

He had his headquarters in a Korean graveyard which was one of the oases in Korea. About midnight the cable came in and it said, "You will proceed to Tokyo where you will advise General Douglas B. MacArthur that he has been relieved of his command." Well, what had happened was that they did not send it to me in Tokyo because they were sure that Willoughby would intercept it, and therefore I could not execute it because then the concern was that General MacArthur, if he knew this was going to happen, would preempt the stage, which he was fully capable of and highly talented enough to do. I have to tell you I admired General MacArthur. Anything you want to say about his ego is correct, but don't ever underestimate the enormous talent of that man. He was an enormously talented man and very, very fair where I was concerned.

An apocryphal story grew up in the Pacific that the UP had asked me what would I have done if I had gotten the cablegram in time. I said, "No problem. It was a presidential order, I would have commandeered the first plane. I would have flown immediately to Tokyo. After hours I would have commandeered an automobile. I would have driven immediately to General MacArthur's quarters and I would have taken the orders, rung the bell, shoved them under the door, and run like hell."

When I got back, Sam Rayburn, who was my friend and a magnificent man, said, "Frank, we always knew you were lucky but we didn't know you had God on your side."

I lived with a great man in Mr. Truman. He surrounded himself with strong men. He was not a brilliant man, he was not a deeply educated man, but he was a man who with great courage, wrapped in the mantle of presidency, achieved a miraculous change, and may go down as the great President of the United States in this century.

QUESTION: Could I ask about the circumstances in the decision to drop the bomb on Hiroshima, which is one of the aspects of his presidency that's always concerned me? You speak of long terms.

MR. PACE: Well, there was great discussion on this at all levels. This was not a presidential quick decision. The decision was that basically without so doing, the war probably would drag on for an unlimited period. There would be far greater loss of Japanese life, far greater loss of American life, far greater incursions in a situation that would not permit an honorable solution. Whether wrong or right, certainly out of it did come a quick termination of war. Certainly it did permit the Japanese, who were people very easily subject to subjugation, to accept General MacArthur; strangely enough I don't believe any other American could have gone over and replaced the emperor and yet it was no step at all for General MacArthur. As a matter of fact he felt a little down-graded. I say all this with a very clear understanding on your part that I admired him. There was no question, however, about the level of his ego. I have come to the conclusion that the decision that was reached there was overall a wise one for civilization. I can tell you some decisions after that time that may have troubled me a little bit more.

QUESTION: What were his own statements about the thought processes he had at the time?

MR. PACE: Almost exactly what I've stated to you. I was a minor actor on the stage when we decided to assume world leadership. The major actors were General Marshall, Dean Acheson, and to a lesser degree Clark Clifford. None of us thought we were qualified for world leadership. We hadn't had the experience, the practice, but all of us knew there wasn't anybody else around. So I don't fault us for that. What I fault us for is not trying to get rid of it as fast as we could after we got it, but you can't take this democracy and lead a free world. But that phrase "leader of the free world" has a lovely ring to it, and it sounds very good in the ears of presidents and secretaries of state, and our effort to get rid of world leadership has been far less than I think the society might have made. All in all, adding up our lack of experience and our original lack of desire to undertake it, I have to say that while we have not done in any sense a classic job, that possibly we rate a B− on how we've handled it since that time.

QUESTION: In light of the high esteem that President Truman is held in now, to what do you attribute his very low popularity during his presidency? I read that in the polls it was as low as 28% at one time.

MR. PACE: That's correct. I think you can attribute it to two things: the first was that President Truman, you must remember, succeeded President Roosevelt, who died disliked very strenuously by a limited number of people but admired broadly by the great mass of the American people. He was a giant who did nothing either to train or bring Mr. Truman into the limelight, so Mr. Truman stepped into the limelight both unprepared and unknown. Early on in his decisions about the war and postwar he won general acceptance and early on he was well received. He did two remarkable things, maybe two of the more remarkable things our country has ever done: the Marshall Plan which restored the health of Europe, a very imaginative and well-carried out plan; and the determination to deal with a very gentle hand with the defeated enemy. That had never been done in the history of man, ergo we have a Germany and a Japan on our side. It would have been a very rough road if you had the kind of smoldering resentment and bitterness you'd had after other wars.

The Roosevelt period had been very hard on the Republican party. There was a very vehement desire to get back into power. The China situation, the China cards were played very, very hard. The failure to support Chiang Kai-shek, who in the light of history was really very questionable in his deserving of support because he ran a very autocratic and a relatively corrupt and certainly very undemocratic regime, but that gave rise to the sense that they were soft on Communism. The attitude toward Taiwan that did not agree to go all out where they were concerned created a general sense of malaise.

Mr. Truman made some mistakes. And of course Dean Acheson's very thoughtless remark, "I will not turn my back on Alger Hiss" did nothing to add to his popularity. Mr. Truman referred to the process as a red herring, that likewise caused people to begin to wonder, and then you reviewed the fact that he had been in the Pendergast machine, and had been a haberdasher, and people began to wonder what kind of a man is he. Finally, he made a lot of unpopular decisions because he thought they were right. That is what moved him down to about 22%, even in his second term after that very spectacular victory.

I remember I was deputy director of the budget. Webb was gone and the President would call in asking about some feature of the budget. He was very much a balanced budget man and very interested in the budget. And after it was over he said, "Frank, we've got them on the run." I said, "What is he sticking in his veins? He must be taking some kind of dope. Nobody can believe he's got them on the run." I don't know if you remember that period, I do vividly. It just wan't any doubt on earth that Thomas E. Dewey was going to win. I had Gabriel Hauge down there determining how the budget ought to be run. I assumed that Gabriel Hauge was going to be running it but he never doubted it at all.

There was humor, a sense of the broad perspective that humor brings to you, of a sense of modesty about yourself, no modesty about the presidency, an ability to say things clearly—these are the things that have come through. This guy was for real and he had courage, and that's why he's where he is today. Thank you for your question.

QUESTION: One more question. The use of military power today and the conceptual use of it in diplomacy seems out of reason to me from my thirty-four years of observation. It seems today there is a vocal ascription to military power which is totally out of bounds with the diplomatic objectives and achievements that we hope for. Would you care to discuss that one for me?

MR. PACE: I have felt that Mr. Reagan's very attractive campaign slogan "Do you want to be inferior to the Russians?" has really dominated the thinking of the administration. It's a marvelous campaign slogan, nobody wants to be inferior to the Russians. Where I find difficulty with it is that first, there is no way we can stay even. When we start doing something the Russians are going to start doing exactly the same thing. If we are even to stay within reach of them, we've got to lower our standard of living. When the American people understand that that is the issue, that's when the ball game stops, and therefore I do not think that the possibility of attaining equality with the Russians lies within the capacity of this democratic society. It is Reagan's thesis and this is possibly correct, probably correct, if you want to negotiate with the Russians you want to negotiate from equal strength. I don't think they respect anything but power. I think that's the name of the game in their life.

My thesis is that we cannot ultimately match them. If I were them, I would absolutely love what Mr. Reagan is doing because it gives me every reason not to do very much for my people, for whom I don't want to do very much because if they get smart enough they're going to get me out of there. And therefore my thesis is that I want to keep them dumb and under control. But once they have got a legitimate position—we're erring in thinking that the U.S. is a peaceful country—then you've got a very legitimate reason to move.

There are not very many attractive tracks here. Disarmament is an important one if it can be made to work. It takes two to tango and I'm not sure about the Russians. A more difficult but more compelling process would be constantly to direct yourself toward separating the Russian people and their leaders. But with their capacity to indoctrinate their young, that is one unthinkably difficult task. I watched a debate in which three young Americans who spoke Russian were debating the Russian position versus the U.S. position, largely it was a very young audience. And the young audience was actually amused, not in a sneering way, they just thought what these young people were saying was silly, the thought that we were peaceful and that they were aggressive. I could see in those faces—this wasn't some sort of a snicker, it was just open disbelief that anything that was said that showed we were peaceful and they were aggressive just didn't make any sense at all. So, you've got a very difficult task, incredibly difficult. I'm not much for explaining why something isn't good unless I've got something a little better. I'm not sure I've got something better.

QUESTION: At an earlier session on President Truman on the presidency, we had a very interesting comment about President Truman's activities during the birth of Israel which I particularly appreciated. And I was wondering if you would comment on that. And I would also like to hear your comments about the Truman-Eisenhower relationship.

MR. PACE: On Israel, Mr. Truman was both dedicated and political. It's possible to be both but he deeply believed there should be a state of Israel. He deeply believed that somewhere there had to be a place for them to be. Certainly he didn't pick the best place, but then I don't know whether there was any better place. Take that aggressive, able group of people and stick them anywhere they are going to get hated pretty quickly. But he deeply believed in it and he established it on the basis that it was right. He was not unaware that the Jewish vote in this society is more important than its numbers. And I'm sure that he was quite satisfied to tie conviction to political advantage.

On his relationship with Mr. Eisenhower, they were very friendly at one time. Incidentally, he was, up to a point, very much an admirer of General MacArthur. You remember he flew halfway across the Pacific rather than order General MacArthur back. In fact he was hopeful that General Eisenhower would run on the Democratic ticket for President and sent Averell Harriman over to discuss that with him. But in the campaign Mr. Truman was what he is, a pure politician. He said, "Frank, every political battle I have I fight with everything I've got, and when it's over I get hold of my opponent and we have a bourbon and branch and say, 'What can we do for the country?'" Pretty lovely philosophy. But he couldn't have a bourbon and branch with Ike. Ike was a military man not a politician, and he saw these attacks from a fellow with whom he had had a good relationship as almost a series of low blows, and he reacted very strongly to that. And the post-election period between Mr. Truman and Mr. Eisenhower was a very unhappy one for Mr. Truman because he still thought very well of Mr. Eisenhower.

It was particularly difficult because I watched him actually reincarnate Herbert Hoover who was still struggling under the Depression era that left the impression that he was bumbling and inadequate, which was inaccurate. He treated him with great respect, brought him to the White House (Mr. Roosevelt never did this), and really brought Mr. Hoover back to where he should have been. Having done that, he felt that being ignored, while he never made any public statements on it, he felt very deeply that somewhere there was a miscarriage of justice.

QUESTION: As I recall you appointed the first civilian general counsel. Was this for institutional reasons or was this because of lack of confidence in the then judge advocate general?

MR. PACE: No. Institutional alone. I couldn't handle this thing with congressional committees through the judge advocate general. It was too much wired into the old Army process. I had to bring in a new man who had no background in this. The Army had a great habit of sweeping things under a rug on the theory that that will stay there, and it just wasn't true. They were forever getting caught with their pants down. I appointed civilian aides in each state and whenever a story appeared on the Army I had this civilian aide investigate it and then go to the editor and say, "This story just isn't true, and I want to tell you why," or say, "Your story is true and you can keep on printing it as long as you want to.'' I had to establish a status with the media and a status with Congress that was compelling in a very difficult period, so I had to appoint a civilian. I appointed my classmate and friend and he was superb.

QUESTION: I'm not sure this is a fair question, if it's not rule it out, Frank.

MR. PACE: Mr. Truman said, "There are no unfair questions, only unfair answers."

QUESTION: You have made a statement with respect to our society vis à vis the fulfillment of its role of world leadership. I think I understood you to say that this is a rocky course and you referred to the free press as one of the obstacles as to why this could not be fulfilled because of the deliberation necessary in the interim in the thought processes. Later you have commented on the enormous effectiveness under the Russian philosophy of indoctrinating youth over there. Would you care to take those two points of view and relate them to where they are going to lead? Are you implying that there is considerable thought that accommodation at any cost is inevitable, and why not now?

MR. PACE: No, I certainly wouldn't want to leave that impression at all. But your question is very penetrating and a thoughtful one.

We have a system that functions superbly in isolation. The founders thought about how they'd take the great riches of this land and develop them for the benefit of all the people while at the same time sustaining a level of freedom and morality, and also avoid tyranny and corruption. They set up a system of checks and balances to ensure that no tyrant would ever take over the U.S.A. and that we would not be the subject of the kind of corruption that was to be seen in Europe. And that system worked so superbly that we've never had a tyrant close to the top of the U.S.A., and in the richest country on earth corruption has been comparatively so minimal it's not worth discussing. But those checks and balances make it enormously difficult for us to move. It makes it very, very difficult for us make decisions. Four or five studies of the presidency have caused me to believe that this most powerful man in the world is indeed a man of very limited power. The relationship of the Congress to bureaucracies is so compelling that the thought that the President manages the government is one that needs very careful reconsideration.

The Soviet system has many cracks in it. They are masters at both indoctrinating their own people and training native troops. What they did to the North Koreans as compared to what we did to the South

Koreans, I'll never forget. But this is a nation that still has a very precarious position. Sometimes the military and the politicians have got to fall out; they can't go right down that road together, in my estimation. They've got countries, like Poland, where they are hated, right next door to them. China will never again mix with the Russians. I do not suggest any inevitability of Russian success. I am merely saying that we have to take a very hard look at what it takes for us to continue to be competitive. We've been competitive because we are so wealthy. I'd have to give us absolute A's on our support of freedom, our recognition of human rights, and our desire, as far as possible, to achieve some equality of economic benefits. On the management of our resources I'd have to give us a C−. And the system is not geared to permit us to bring that C− up. On foreign policy, as I said, I'd probably give us a B−; the system does not permit us to bring that up. I'm talking in very loose, pragmatic terms just for the purpose of trying to answer a very difficult question reasonably well.

The long stretch is for us, if we organize ourselves, to take care of it. That system cannot make it, not just because it's evil but because it's inadequate. If you're there, as I was on a tour, you cannot help but be impressed with the fact that even their efforts to copy us are inadequate. They recognize that under the facade of Communism they have to practice a form of capitalism. And while no one knows, I am honestly a true believer that the long pull is for us, but what I am pressing for is just to recognize that that pull is not easy, that that pull is very difficult and that there are better ways than we are doing it right now to get there.

MR. THOMPSON: Mr. Secretary, we have a tradition in this place that if he feels like it, we ask our most distinguished of all University of Virginia scholars to either ask a question or make a comment, Dumas Malone.

MR. PACE: You can permit him to do both.

DUMAS MALONE: I met Mr. Truman once when he spoke here and I had the pleasure of having lunch with him beforehand. I was very much impressed with what you said about his taking the long view. I had recently been reading his memoirs and I think almost the first thing I said to him was that I had greatly admired his interest in history. He liked history. And I said, "I was especially impressed with what you said about McCarthy, that it made you think of the alien and sedition acts," and he said "That's the first thing I thought of." So I think he took the long view. I liked him very much indeed. So that's my contribution.

QUESTION: Do you agree entirely with Harry Truman that there were too many Byrds in the Senate?

MR. PACE: No, no. I have to say to you I was a deep admirer of Senator Byrd, Senior. I didn't know Senator Byrd, Junior at all well, but I did know him. You see, I have historically been a fiscal conservative and basically a liberal on human rights, and that means that you have to strike a compromise always. Senator Byrd saw way back then the enormous danger of ever letting this budgetary process get out of hand. And with him in the Senate we just weren't going to let it get out of hand. It was indeed the old Southern senators who really kept the seesaw in balance instead of letting it get too far under, say, Mr. Roosevelt. It was Lyndon Johnson who undermined that old Southern strong coalition that stood for the very careful utilization of our resources. So, as a very long answer to a very short question, for me there weren't enought Byrds in the Senate.

QUESTION: Were the differences between Byrd and Truman really deep and troublesome?

MR. PACE: No, no. Not at all. Senator Byrd took a different point of view from Mr. Truman. Mr. Truman's political statements very rarely reflected his personal feelings. I think if you sat down with a bourbon and branch, he'd inform you he thought Harry Byrd was a pretty good fellow. He referred to my senator as Woolbright, and then later as Halfbright, and yet he did not dislike Bill Fulbright. He just liked to designate what he thought he was.

MR. THOMPSON: Well, thank you very much for being with us, and most of all we thank Secretary Pace for an illuminating, fair-minded, balanced, and enormously perceptive presentation of the Truman presidency and of President Truman as a person. Thank you very much.

THE INFLUENCE OF
HARRY S TRUMAN ON THE
MARSHALL PLAN*
W. Averell Harriman

WILSON: We'd like to get at some of the questions relating to your experiences, to your career. You may recall at the time we gave the presentation at the last library board meeting, we tried to describe some of the problems we'd encountered, particularly the problem of how the written record has led us astray or can lead historians astray on occasion. We thought that perhaps to pose you the question that bothered us most:

> One of the most voluminous subject files of information about the war-time planning for the postwar world and the immediate postwar period deals with this question of the State Department's efforts, and the effort of the Treasury Department, to create an economic open world—Cordell Hull's idea. We'd like to have you react to that—describe how that might have come to you.

*Governor Harriman's contribution to this volume is based on an interview in 1971 taped for the Truman Library with Richard D. McKinzie and Theodore A. Wilson in Washington, D.C. Governor Harriman and the Harry S. Truman Library have kindly given permission for its inclusion in this book.

HARRIMAN: I think there are telegrams that may or may not be available, which indicated that I very much had in mind the need to give Europe substantial aid after the war, after Lend-Lease was over. As the matter of fact, I felt it should also include countries not involved in Lend-Lease—whose economies would be completely disorganized. UNRRA was not enough. Europe would need not just food, but also raw materials and working capital to get the wheels of commerce going again. It wasn't just rebuilding factories; it was getting all the machinery of trade and commerce going again. Since they were without any foreign exchange, I felt it necessary for us to do something. I was particularly conscious of it, because I knew the condition Britain would be in, converting from wartime to peacetime economy.

I was very much concerned over our failure to come to an agreement with the British on continuing Lend-Lease assistance after the war was over. In fact, when Oliver Littleton was in the United States, I think it was around 1943, I urged him to consider the needs of the postwar period, but apparently he was under instructions from [Sir Winston] Churchill not to do it, or didn't want to do it. He had immediate wartime emergency needs. This was the period when I used all the influence I had to get the British to abandon their export trade, and as much as possible convert all of their manufacturing facilities to the immediate needs of the war, including civilian, as well as military requirements.

I felt a certain responsibility to help the British, as I had urged the British to abandon their export trade and convert to war production. You will remember, the British got most of their raw materials and half their food from abroad. Their ability to buy necessities from abroad was essential. We did give the British a three billion seven or eight hundred million dollar loan. But I was very much upset that we didn't extend the principle of Lend-Lease into the postwar period.

As far as the Russians were concerned, I felt the reverse; they had adequate gold, if they wanted to buy, and they weren't dependent upon international trade. I felt they were more self-sufficient. The Russians obtained a number of plants under Lend-Lease, which had been authorized by Washington, that I thought were not justified for their war effort. They wanted them for postwar use. I had a friendly feeling towards the Russians, but I felt they didn't need these plants. The Russians often took advantage of Lend-Lease. On one occasion, I think it was the time [Henry] Wallace came to the Soviet Union when we went to the Golena gold fields, Wallace discovered a dredge which we were supposed to have given the Russians to deepen one of the harbors in the Pacific. But, we found the Russians using it to dredge for gold. Well, they received this dredge under Lend-Lease.

It didn't rest well with me that they had deceived us in that way. We never knew fully what they were doing. The British we knew; and it was very clear that the whole of Europe would be weakened, and that Communism—without help—would take over. I'm sure that was one of the reasons why [Joseph] Stalin broke his agreements, because the situation looked too good in Western Europe for a Communist takeover. I think Stalin was convinced he could move into Western Europe. He was undoubtedly told by leaders in the Communist parties in Italy and France that their organizations were very strong; that with some help they would be able to take over Italy and France; and I think they would have done so if it hadn't been for the Marshall Plan.

So, my reports to Washington started in the autumn of '44 and '45, with some telegrams, in which my general point of view was directed toward the above. It never occurred to me that we would have as grandiose a program as the Marshall Plan, but I felt that we had to do something to save Europe from economic disaster which would encourage the Communist takeover.

MCKINZIE: You did not then get a great deal of Cordell Hull's view that after the war there would be a remarkable amount of commerce —normal commerce?

HARRIMAN: No. My views were just the reverse. I was not at all in sympathy with this idea. You know, I ran the Marshall Plan in Paris. I and a small staff had control of the operations in Europe. We were pressing for EPU, European Payments Union. We had a lot of opposition from the Treasury Department on this and not much cooperation from State. I think their economic approach was just the reverse of ours. We were talking about really getting Europe on its feet. It was our hope that there would be a breakdown of trade barriers in Europe first, and then eventually a breakdown internationally, which would help increase trade with Europe.

I knew this would mean a temporary sacrifice for the United States to some extent. We had a lot of trouble with the Department of Treasury; they were not particularly keen on the European Payments Union. Our whole concept of the unification of Europe was that it would first contribute to economic unification. Then, we hoped to secure an economic-military unity and finally a political unity. In the first instance, it was obvious that theoretically at least there would be some sacrifice in trade to the United States, but in the long run the buying power of Europe would increase so greatly that we would gain.

WILSON: How are we to explain the continuation of this universalist philosophy in places like the Treasury? Was it because they were idealists or unrealistic, or was it because . . .

HARRIMAN: Well, they were working on GATT [General Agreement on Trade and Tariffs]. Everybody seemed concerned about GATT. That's one trouble with bureaucracy. Bureaucrats are like hunting dogs. They are down a certain scent, and they stick to that scent, even though there may be some better scents in one direction or another. I use the word "scents" in a double meaning.

WILSON: Yes.

HARRIMAN: I was all for the ideals, but I knew we were not in a position to get the ideal in the European Recovery Program. I was quite ready to accept certain restrictions on the United States. After all, there was a great dollar shortage. It was quite clear that the more prosperous Europe became, the more business there would be in the United States. My whole experience in banking showed me that. The biggest trade that Germany and Britain had was with each other, in the prewar period; I think I'm right in that. Two highly industrialized nations had the most trade with each other, and it wasn't tariff policies alone that made trade relations better for both of them. So, I had a different view than this idealistic theory of simply breaking down barriers. I was much more involved in the practical problem of getting Europe back on its feet, and giving it an opportunity to move ahead—move forward—and everything we did was in that direction. EPU was an example; we had a lot of troubles with the Treasury in putting EPU through, the European Payments Union . . .

MCKINZIE: Yes.

HARRIMAN: . . . and yet the European Payments Union, I'm satisfied, was a thing which made the Marshall Plan a success and made it possible for Europe to move rapidly after the Marshall Plan was finished. And I think in a sense it was one of the things that made it possible for Europe to become viable more rapidly. I was fighting for EPU; it had a good deal of support from the French, the Italians, and the Belgians.

The British were very much opposed to it; they had a great deal of difficulty. Sir Stafford Cripps was adamantly against it. They thought it would interfere with their sterling area; there were a lot of complications. It was hard to fully understand why they were opposed to it. One thing about Cripps was that after he made an agreement he always did a little better than he said he would. It was very tough to get him to agree to something, but after he came to an agreement he was very cooperative.

I look upon these theories, which were held in the Treasury and to some extent in the Department of State, as irritants against doing the job which we were trying to do and which we did in spite of their positions. I think the record shows that EPU was the most specific case. Yet the whole preamble of the second authorization act for the Marshall Plan showed the direction Congress was ready to take about breaking down barriers within Europe. I was anxious that it shouldn't be just a customs union—a customs union which would exclude the United States. I wanted to see more fundamental understandings about greater integration than simply a customs union. That I think is happening, although some people call European integration more of a customs union that I do. I think it's more fundamental. The military aspects are also very important.

Actually I'd had a certain amount of experience in Europe in the inter-war period, as a banker, and I was also a member of the Board of Directors of the International Chamber of Commerce. I remember meeting in one of the executive committee meetings in Paris. I went there because I happened to be there; I was the only American of any prominence there—of any of the directors. They had a staff. One evening I remember that I met with the leading bankers and industrialists of the principal countries. I remember the British and German, the French—I can't remember who else was there. It was quite a small dinner—it was a private dinner. Yet, they took the International Chamber of Commerce more seriously than we did, and there were very important men present. I asked them why they thought that the United States was moving ahead as we were in the mid-twenties, you remember, whereas Europe was stagnant with built-in unemployment. They said it was because we had a continent of free trade.

And I said, "Well, if that's the case, why don't you with all your influence in different countries make the changes that are necessary to get freer trade in Europe?"

The answer was that unless there was a military understanding, freedom of trade could not exist. Because there wasn't a military understanding of some kind, every country, for its own security, demanded to be as autarkic as possible. And I think one man said, "From castings to forged big guns, to buttons on the uniform." I remember some of the details.

So, I went into the Marshall Plan with the idea that both economic and military considerations had to be taken into account. This is one of the differences I had with [Paul] Hoffman. He wanted to limit it to economic goals alone, and I was very keen to see the NATO treaty become more of a reality, remembering this experience in the inter-war period. Now that isn't an answer directly to your question, but it does show that we looked upon military integration and economic integration as supporting each other.

We did everything we could, of course, to develop the OEEC as a vital organization. We were—I think I can use the word "I"—was determined that we would get the Europeans to divide aid. I had a horror of fourteen countries coming to the United States with their front feet in the trough. I thought the net result of that would be that we would have fourteen enemies of the United States and fourteen enemies among each other, because of the jealousy that would come.

How could you justify giving Holland twice the amount of money that you gave Belgium? Well, finally, I put it up to them. They said that they couldn't do it; it would destroy them. I said they had to do it. And I finally got support from Hoffman on it. We did get them to divide the aid, and that was one of the things that made the organization successful. We were dealing with the practical realities of the ghastly situation that existed in Europe when we took over. I don't know if you've ever had a full picture of what Europe was in the winter of 1947.

MCKINZIE: We have done some considerable work on it.

HARRIMAN: Well, you know how desperate the situations were. I didn't get into it until April. I went over there the first part of May, and I discovered the British had been very successful in laying down the organization of the OEEC. A young, brilliant economist, Robert Marjolin, headed OEEC, but he had little political prestige in the beginning. It took me a year to get an agreement on a permanent chairman of the ministerial committee of OEEC. We wanted to get [Paul-Henri] Spaak, but we got [Dirk U.] Stikker who was a fine fellow and a very able fellow. (Spaak was a little too active. The British opposition to him was mostly because he was a Socialist.) Everything we did was to strengthen European unity. The European Payments Union was an effective move. It was very much in the direction of the integration of Europe.

On the sidelines we had Jean Monnet, who worked on the specifics of the coal and steel community. I kept in touch with him. Any agreement between [Robert] Schuman and [Dr. Konrad] Adenauer was of major significance. I was never directly involved in what they were doing, but these were related to what we were trying to do. So these were the things that interested us, and not the ideological trade concepts advanced by Mr. Hull. I'm very much in favor of as much free trade as you can get in the world, but I've never looked upon it as an ideological concept. You've got to move in that direction, but also deal with realities.

WILSON: We have the impression from the documentation that a tinge of this ideological idealism may have crept into the Washington office of the ECA—about how to proceed with European integration. That is, there was pressure for rather large scale commitments on the part of the European nations to work together, and that perhaps you were rather more interested in going a step at a time again. Is that correct?

HARRIMAN: Well, I think it was true. ECA was separate from State. We didn't clash so much with State as we did with Treasury. Of course you had to get Treasury's agreement on some of these things— God knows why—but we did. The economic side of State was not tough; the financial side of the Treasury was tough. General Marshall and Bob [Robert] Lovett, and Acheson were all for the Marshall Plan, and offered to give us cooperation. One man in the Treasury with whom we had the most difficulty was kept on by Eisenhower when he took over. I've forgotten his name. Perhaps you can find out who he was.

MCKINZIE: [Lieutenant Colonel C.H.] Bonesteel?

HARRIMAN: No, no, no. This is Treasury. Assistant Secretary of the Treasury. No, no, Bonesteel was all right. He was with me in Paris. We got full cooperation from Bob Lovett when he was under secretary, from General Marshall, of course, and from Dean Acheson, when he became Secretary of State in 1949.

   I'm making myself plain that these economic theories were not actually the main consideration, whereas in the Treasury, they were.

WILSON: What about the role of Will [William L.] Clayton, at the time of the origins of the Marshall Plan?

HARRIMAN: I never had very much to do with him, as related to the Marshall Plan. I don't know what role he played. I was Secretary of Commerce at that time. What contacts I had with State, and the Marshall Plan in those days, were with Dean Acheson. I had a certain amount to do in connection with Greece and Turkey. I remember the Marshall Plan came along very fast after that.

WILSON: Yes, yes.

HARRIMAN: I've heard other people speak about the role that Clayton played. I think the book by [Joseph M.] Jones is probably about as accurate as anything available on the Marshall Plan.

MCKINZIE: *Fifteen Weeks.*

HARRIMAN: *Fifteen Weeks.* As Secretary of Commerce, I had many talks with Acheson, but there are very few records of our conversations. We talked about Greece and Turkey, and I was in agreement with a good many things on it all. But I've no records of it, because they were talks among two friends.

I was a couple years ahead of Dean in school, in college, and we knew each other very well. He was one of the driving forces in developing the Truman Doctrine first, and then the Marshall Plan.

General Marshall was one of the slowest to recognize we were going to have difficulties with the Soviet Union. He, as well as General [Dwight D.] Eisenhower, tried his best to get along with Stalin. One of the most important facts to discredit the revisionists who contended we were responsible for the cold war was the attitude of General Marshall and General Eisenhower. It's very interesting that these two men were among the last to agree that we couldn't get along with Stalin. General Marshall didn't come to that conclusion until after he made his terrific effort at the Moscow Conference in '47.

[Walter] Bedell Smith, who was my successor as ambassador to the Soviet Union, was very close to Marshall during the war. He told me about his talk with General Marshall in the winter of 1946, before he [Smith] went to Moscow, when he was reviewing with General Marshall the list of people he ought to see. General Marshall then, of course, was—I guess he was still Chief of Staff of the Army, or was he in '46?

WILSON: No. He just retired.

HARRIMAN: Just retired. Well anyway, he didn't call anybody by his first name. He said, "Of course, you've got to see Harriman, and he will have a lot to tell you about them. But he had such a rough time there, you want to discount a bit his appraisal of the situation." That was in '46. It wasn't until March-April of 1947 at the Foreign Ministers' Moscow Conference which he attended that General Marshall finally gave up hope for coming to an understanding with Stalin.

I tell the story, not to gossip, but to show you we had very important sources within our government that were still determined. And it's interesting . . .

MCKINZIE: Determined for conciliation?

HARRIMAN: Yes. It's still '47. I've never gone over the records of that meeting, but I guess he had a pretty rough time didn't he?

MCKINZIE: Oh, yes.

WILSON: Very frustrating time.

HARRIMAN: It was the same way with General Eisenhower. The reason for it was that Stalin kept his military commitments, and neither Marshall nor Eisenhower were involved in the political phase. As you know, Stalin attacked the Germans after the Normandy landing, and if the Russians hadn't attacked at that time we would have been in real trouble, because there were some two hundred German divisions on the Russian front, and about thirty mobile divisions in Western Europe. In addition, there were about fifty satellite divisions on the Russian front, and thirty-odd mobile German divisions. This made a deep impression on Marshall and Eisenhower. They were convinced that since Stalin kept his word on vital military commitments he'd keep his word on the political matters.

You asked what my relation with Wallace was: Henry Wallace, when he was Secretary of Agriculture, came to Russia while I was ambassador. We were good personal friends, but I disagreed with him on many things. But he was made Secretary of Agriculture. In any event, I was working for the NRA and we had common problems in the early thirties. Anyway, I got one of the nicest letters I've ever gotten from anybody when I took his place as Secretary of Commerce in 1946. There was no personal vindictiveness or negative feeling towards me at all.

WILSON: Yes.

HARRIMAN: Wallace was very sincere. He was very much of a dreamer about Communism, and about the Russians and about other things. He was very sincere in his convictions. He had some people around him that may have been misguided or that were misguided. Whether they were fellow travelers or Communist party members, I have no idea. But his attitudes were very sincere. How much of Wallace's Madison Square Garden foreign policy speech Mr. Truman read or took in, I have no idea. I've never really been able to find that out.

MCKINZIE: Well, we had various people look at this speech—scan it—but we can't tell how much the President actually saw.

HARRIMAN: But why weren't some of the differences with [James F.] Byrnes' policies noticeable by that time? Byrnes was very strongly suspicious of the Russians. In the beginning, in early meetings, he learned the hard way from making certain mistakes that dealing with the Russians was quite different from what he first thought. I don't know why the White House staff didn't realize what his speech was, do you? I never tried to find out.

MCKINZIE: There was a little bit of fuzziness about lines of responsibility, I think, in the White House staff on such matters as that. It wasn't until much later that the White House staff got very concerned about the content of speeches. I think they did appoint someone after that.

WILSON: But it is also suggested that Byrnes overreacted to this, because he felt unsure about it.

HARRIMAN: Byrnes may have overreacted; again, let's read that speech over and think about it—the Wallace speech. I think you will find that it wasn't all that bad or all that at variance with Truman's policy. I think that's what may be true; I'd like to check that, and if I have an opinion on it I'll get it to you.

MCKINZIE: Very good.

HARRIMAN: Now you go back to the next question you asked.

WILSON: What were the circumstances of your taking on the Harriman Committee [President's Committee on Foreign Aid] assignment?

HARRIMAN: I know that the President wanted to have a thorough analysis. He knew how to deal with Congress. Everybody gives General Marshall credit for the Marshall Plan. I don't want to take one iota of credit for the Marshall Plan, but there is one man who is responsible for the Marshall Plan and that was Harry S. Truman, because he developed the plan and got it through Congress. He got vigorous support but he got it through Congress. Anyway, I have no idea exactly how these three committees were developed.

There was the [Edwin] Nourse Committee, which was the Committee of Economic Advisers. Then there was the Committee on Resources, which was headed by . . .

MCKINZIE: Julius Krug.

HARRIMAN: . . . who was then Secretary of the Interior.

This [the Harriman Committee] was a very strangely organized committee, because you had a Secretary of Commerce as chairman of it, with all the other members being private citizens drawn from industry, commerce, banking, finance, the intellectual world, labor, Congress. It was a group with very wide opinions. Who got the idea of putting me in as chairman, I don't know; you'll have to find that out from somebody else. I think at the time, you see this was 1947, I was still considered more of a businessman than a politician. I don't know why. I don't know who was the man that made the decision, maybe Dean Acheson. I don't know. Have you seen anything?

WILSON: We've seen some early memoranda on the development of the idea. One, there is a Policy Planning Staff memorandum, apparently responding to a speech by [Senator Arthur H.] Vandenberg on or about the 14th of June, in which he says the Marshall speech was a fine idea and now we need a bipartisan group—a blue-ribbon group —to see whether it's feasible or not.

HARRIMAN: I know Vandenberg was called in on the composition of this group. I got along very well with Vandenberg. We were very good friends. I had respect for him. I think it really was mutual. He was responsible for the additions of two men. One was Owen D. Young and the other was Bob [Senator Robert M., Jr.] LaFollette. He felt the selection was not sufficiently wide or popular. He knew the people; he didn't question their ability or anything.

WILSON: Yes, yes.

HARRIMAN: He was looking for people whose names would carry with them a stamp of public approval—the stamp that would gain public approval. So, I remember he added those two names, Young and LaFollette. He told me he thought it wasn't quite representative enough. They were very capable men, all of them. He always told me that it was rapport that made it possible for him to get the legislation through Congress.

WILSON: Yes.

HARRIMAN: I was lucky in getting Dick [Richard M., Jr.] Bissell as executive secretary. He was one of the most outstanding economists I've ever known. He had the courage of his convictions. To put forward such fantastic conclusions as Dick did was a tremendously courageous thing to do. I'd say it turned out right; we actually hit well within the figures. We had a very good group and we divided up in seven different committees.

Bob LaFollette wrote the chapter on America's interest in Europe. I don't know why it received as much acceptance as it did, except that it was written in layman's language, so that the . . .

WILSON: Yes. Very clear.

HARRIMAN: . . . press understood what we were talking about. We had a press conference which went very well, in which Bissell and Bob LaFollette and I talked to the press together. Bissell had a very skillful way of making very complicated things simple. Most of Congress could make very simple things complicated (but that's not on the record).

My contribution to the committee was that I was the chairman and tried to keep people's nerves down, because there were some people opposed to it. They just couldn't believe that we would spend 17 billion, which was fantastic to them. We never got a vote on the report as a whole. Agreement was obtained from the seven subcommittees, covering seven aspects of the report. We had to get this report out fast, because Congress was about to meet in a session.

So, I called up each one of the men, and I said, "We're going to issue this report. You haven't had a chance to read it, but each one of you has agreed to your segment of it." A number of members, including Bob LaFollette, read the whole report and approved it. Then I said, "We'll have to send this forward as the report of the committee and if there is any aspect of it that any member does not approve when he reads it, he can make a minority objection."

Well, the press reaction was so tremendously favorable that the opponents who disagreed didn't come to the last meeting. By the way, I said this at the last meeting—none of them had a chance to read it all, or I should say some of them had. That's the way we got it through.

Vandenberg later told me that it was that report that was really more help than anything else in getting legislation on the Marshall Plan through Congress. There was a lot of work done in our State Department, subsequently. But the important fact was that the report was adopted by our members without any objection by an outside group. For some reason or other, even though I was Secretary of Commerce, I had not been contaminated, sufficiently contaminated, to be excluded. I was, of course, one of the many people who had worked for the government in wartime, you know . . .

MCKINZIE: Oh, yes.

HARRIMAN: . . . that wartime service wasn't considered as tarring you with the political brush.

MCKINZIE: Governor Harriman, we don't want to go longer than the time you had allotted for us . . .

TRUMAN: AN APPRAISAL
Francis Heller

It was a spring day in 1953 in Kansas City, Missouri. As the noon hour came around, the towering office buildings in the heart of the city's business district began to disgorge the daily flood of clerks and executives on their way to lunch. Among those passing through the doors of the Federal Reserve Bank building at the corner of Grand Avenue and 10th Street was a group of three men moving along in obviously animated conversation. They looked to be in their late fifties or early sixties and nothing about them set them off in the noonday crowd. Yet passers-by stopped to look, and here and there one could hear a querying "That *is* him, isn't it?" As the three turned east on 10th Street, a barber waved at the trio from his shop; a man walked up to the man in the middle, shook his hand and said, "Good to have you back in town, Harry!"

One block to the east, the three men walked into the restaurant of the Hotel Pickwick. Although it was not one of the leading hotels of the city (it adjoined and merged into the bus terminal), the Pickwick enjoyed good patronage at lunch; its roast beef sandwiches were justly renowned. The *maître d'hôtel* met the trio at the door and escorted them to a reserved table. At the next table four men rose and came over to shake hands. "Mr President, welcome home," one said, while the others introduced themselves. A waitress appeared to take orders, but before she could do so, other guests in the restaurant were crowded around to shake hands with Harry Truman. Another waitress had passed the word to the kitchen staff and white-hatted cooks and aproned dishwashers soon began to mingle with the men in business suits who wanted to greet the man who until a few weeks ago had been the President of the United States.

Harry S. Truman never ate lunch that day. It was his first attempt to mingle with the public as a private citizen; he learned that, once having been President, he could never again be an ordinary citizen. Nineteen years later, walking along the corridor of a local hospital to which he was temporarily confined, other patients would hail him in much the same manner. It never quite ceased to amaze him.

For Truman thought of himself primarily as a citizen who, being called to do his duty, did it as best he knew how. Yes, he had held the highest office in the land, but he continued to view that office almost with awe. Characteristically, he insisted that the museum which is part of the library holding his papers should focus its displays not on him but on the Office of the President. Characteristically also, when he agreed to have some of his post-presidential speeches and lectures published in book form, he asked that the book be titled *Mr. Citizen*. Until illness confined him to his home, he would take particular pride and pleasure in brief appearances before groups of school children visiting the Truman Library when, without fail, he would finish his remarks with the admonition to the young people to cherish and to use the privileges given to them as citizens of the United States.

Truman saw himself, first and foremost, as what he believed a good citizen should be. The world may have seen him as a statesman, conferring with Churchill and Stalin, proclaiming the bold ventures of aid to Greece and Turkey, of Point Four, of North Atlantic unity; political sophisticates in Kansas City might recall, with unconcealed disapproval, that his rise in politics was owed to the "machine" of "Boss" Pendergast. Harry Truman saw his career in terms so uncomplicated that political pundits might be unwilling to credit them fully. Truman, however, was consistent throughout his public life: he did what he did because he believed it to be right.

In recent years, so-called "revisionist" historians have turned their attention to the Truman era in American history and many of them have produced reassessments comparable to the book review that deplores that the author did not write a different book.

Truman is both impatient with and tolerant of the critics. He would grant, especially to those too young to have lived through the period themselves as adults, the right to be critical but he could get testy with those who would not credit his own explanations as honest and candid. Thus, as he was engaged in the preparation of his memoirs, a professional historian had been brought in to assist him; when, six months later, I was asked to take this gentleman's place, one of my first queries was to find out where he had gone wrong. The explanation given me provided an excellent introduction to Truman's thinking: the professor simply refused to accept Truman's statement to him that he, Truman, had seen the employment of the atomic bomb solely in terms of weaponry and not of ethics; Truman had grown weary of the repetition of the question. To him, the matter had been uncomplicated then—it was the quickest means to bring the war to an end—and it had remained uncomplicated.

Truman's memoirs are full of explanations which the revisionists reject. Though few persons have had the opportunity to discuss the recent historical writings with him, it stands to reason that he is not upset by the wave of new critics. For one, as a long practising politician he would expect it. His statement that "If you can't stand the heat, stay out of the kitchen" has become an oft-quoted truism. For another, Truman had always been a devoted reader of history and had come to appreciate the relativity of historical judgement.

He made this point to me, again with telling simplicity, shortly after the first volume of his memoirs had come off the press in late 1955. He was then still occupying the office suite in the Federal Reserve Bank building, in one room of which I had worked while the memoirs were being prepared. I found this room filled literally from wall to wall with stacks of copies of the book. Rose Conway, his long-time devoted secretary, explained that people from all over the United States had been sending the former President their copies of the memoirs with requests that he return them with his autograph. She was concerned, she added, because so few of the senders had provided return postage; at fourteen cents apiece (not counting wrapping costs) it would cost Mr. Truman over a hundred dollars to do the requested favours!

By that time, Mr. Truman had come out of his office and invited me to join him there. Quite naturally, I commented on the accumulation of books I had just seen. Truman said he could not quite understand why people were seeking his autograph; indeed, he was still surprised at the number of books that had been sold in the few short weeks since publication. He repeated a sentiment I had heard him express several times before: "All I wanted to do was to put it down on paper for history!" He was, he knew, no Winston Churchill when it came to writing; so why this interest in his memoirs?

I ventured to suggest that for most Americans the years since the Second World War had been years filled with national and international drama and that there would be many who—regardless of whether or not they had approved of all that he, Truman, had done as President—would want to know what these events looked like from the vantage point of the man who had had to make the crucial decisions.

Truman's response revealed that he understood the dynamics of historical forces. (To appreciate this statement, one needs to recall that in the final year of the Truman administration scandals involving gifts of mink coats and deep freezers had touched some of his close associates; Truman's appointment secretary was even then serving a prison sentence growing out of these revelations.) "If," he said after a pause, "it turns out that I was right in ordering the atomic bomb dropped on Hiroshima, and that I was right in proclaiming the Greek-Turkish Aid Doctrine and initiating the Marshall Plan, in resisting the Berlin blockade, and most importantly in ordering the resistance in Korea—if these were decisions that history will say were right because they turned out to have the right consequences, then people aren't going to spend many chapters writing about deep freezers and mink coats. But if it turns out—God protect us—that all these things were wrong, then people are going to take every small thing that can be criticized and make a rope out of it for me."

A critic would readily point out that there is a contradiction in this, essentially relativist, view of historical judgement and the frequent invocation of history as a source of certain knowledge that is to be found at frequent intervals in his recollection of his presidential years. History had always been his favourite reading and he evidently had a flair for the retention of dates and facts. On the other hand, speculations about the nature of history or the problems of historiography were of little interest to him. He accepted the traditional mainstream of history as authoritative and, quite plainly, drew from it for support and reassurance.

The magnificent isolation of the American presidency makes it, of course, almost essential for the man who occupies the office to place himself in the context of "the judgement of history." It is, quite possibly, the major balancing element he can use in the face of the unrelenting pressures of the job. Not surprisingly, allusions to the judgement of history run through the public utterances of virtually all the Presidents (e.g. Lincoln: "The world will very little note nor long remember . . . "; F.D.R.'s "day that shall live in infamy," to cite only the best known). Not only was Truman no exception, but he came to the tasks of the presidency feeling that history was a mainstay of his intellectual resources. Not only those who knew him as senator and President attest to his preoccupation, but so do his family and friends and associates from earlier years.

A major thrust of the kind of historical books which the young Harry Truman had so avidly perused was what some scholars have described as the concept of "Manifest Destiny," the notion that America had a predestined role to fulfill. If, in its earlier manifestations, this idea had served to justify continental expansion, by the late decades of the nineteenth century it had assumed the ideological qualities which Woodrow Wilson would later express in his Fourteen Points. Truman, by his own description, grew up as what would later be described a "Wilsonian Democrat." He believed that America had a mission, a responsibility which it could not shirk. He volunteered for service in the First World War because he believed that it was right to do so; thirty years later he would propose a concept of worldwide aid for much the same reasons.

The First World War marked a watershed in the life of Harry Truman. Biographies of historical personages normally devote much time to the early years, and, typically, the record of early achievement. But a *Who's Who* sketch of Harry S. Truman contains next to nothing on the first thirty-three years of his life. The first event noted usually is "Commanded Battery D, 129th Field Artillery in First World War." Truman himself never failed to highlight the importance he attached to this experience and gave it visible expression when he had the surviving members of the unit brought to Washington to take a place of honour in the ceremonies of Inauguration Day, 1949.

Interestingly enough, some of the persons who admiringly pointed to the importance of the PT-109 experience in the life of John F. Kennedy would speak disdainfully of Truman's pride in Battery D. In part, this may have been due to the dramatic qualities of Kennedy's exploits as against the unspectacular service typical of the ground forces; in part, it may be attributable to the fact that the National Guard was never seen in a glamour role among the military organizations of the United States.

Truman had first joined the National Guard in 1905, at the age of twenty-one. "There were," he reports in his memoirs, "about sixty men in the organization, and most of them were very fine fellows who worked in banks and stores around town and who would go out to a rented armoury once a week and pay a quarter for the privilege of drilling." Truman himself worked in a bank, as a bookkeeper at the modest salary of sixty dollars a month. He was, in many ways, typical of the men who joined the guard: they were clerks, journeymen, professional apprentices—a cross section of the lower middle class. (An exception to this generalization were a few militia units on the eastern seaboard where historic tradition provided high social status.)

Although the militia tradition has deep roots in the United States (witness its specific confirmation in the Bill of Rights, Amendment II), the inadequacy of a volunteer force of part-time citizen-soldiers, as an instrument of national defence had been demonstrated time and again, most recently in the Spanish-American War. As it had after each such experience with the militia, Congress sought to remedy the situation by legislation. Thus the act of 1903 for the first time provided that the "organized militia," i.e. the National Guard, would receive arms and equipment from the army for training. More importantly, it stipulated that a National Guard unit, to qualify for support from the national government, had to hold twenty-five drill or target practice sessions a year and participate in a five-day encampment each summer. In practice, however, both equipment and money were slow in coming and National Guard training continued at a rather low level. Training sessions tended to be overshadowed by the socializing that traditionally followed. The fact that the guard elected its officers and non-commissioned officers tended to reinforce the social aspects of guard activity.

It was not until 1916 that the officers elected by guard units were required to pass qualifying tests and meet criteria of physical fitness. This change, coming as it did on the eve of America's entry into the First World War, probably did little to change the character of the guard until mobilization put the new scheme to the test. Many National Guard officers proved deficient on one ground or the other; Harry S. Truman did very well indeed.

Apparently all his previous guard activity had been of a kind to qualify him as a sergeant. When his fellow soldiers elected him a first lieutenant, he had, in his own words, "a tremendous amount of work to do." Army records show that he did it exceedingly well. By the time his unit reached the front lines in France in July 1918, he was a captain and in command of Battery D. By the time he returned to civilian life in 1919, his ability to provide leadership had stood the test.

The years immediately after the war included some setbacks which were to receive frequent mention by critics and opponents in later years, most notably the financial failure of the menswear store in 1922. What should attract more attention is the contrast in career orientation between the pre-war and the post-war years. Before the military service period, Harry Truman is a bank clerk, then tends the family farm, embarks on a few, generally unsuccessful, ventures in business; he is a faithful member of the Masons as he is of the National Guard, but in all he is follower rather than leader. After the war he not only accepts, but to a degree seeks, the opportunity to serve the public and readily assumes proffered responsibility. He retains a reserve commission in the Army and becomes one of the organizers of the Reserve Officers Association. He begins to move quickly through the advanced degrees of Masonry and is deputy grand master of Missouri by 1924. He runs for public office and serves as one of three members of his county's governing board. His rise into the political arena is at least partly due to the fact that the veterans of Battery D are a ready nucleus of a personal following.

Survivors of that World War organization have, understandably, been queried about the roots of this loyalty. Their responses vary, of course, considerably but what they have in common might be summarized thus: We came to know Harry Truman as a man of common touch and uncommon dependability; if he told us he would do something, we knew that it would be done; as one of them put it, "He always gave more than he asked."

In his years in the White House, Truman would often be criticized because of the preferment he allegedly gave to "cronies," and "cronyism in the White House" was a favourite target of the opposition. At the extreme, it was charged that the recognition of the state of Israel was due to the intervention of the President's erstwhile partner in the ill-fated menswear venture, Eddie Jacobson. Anecdotes about the President's willingness to "help a friend" were being circulated by friend and foe alike.

At the same time, Truman tended to be chary of demands on him, especially if they were couched in terms of obligations owed. He had enjoyed strong support from organized labour when he ran for re-election as senator in 1940, but he reacted with immediate resentment when a high-ranking labour leader, invoking this record of support, sought to influence his decision on the naming of a new Chief Justice in 1946. There is no question that he owed his first success in the political arena to the "machine" of the Pendergasts; but when it was suggested to him that he should, in return as it were, award some lucrative road construction contracts to the Pendergasts and their friends, he flatly said no. He would give—but he would not be dictated to. Tom Pendergast later was found guilty of income tax evasion and went to prison; but Truman knew him as a friend and—though it scandalized the sophisticates—attended his funeral.

The examples could easily be multiplied. What they confirm is that

Truman took a remarkably uncomplicated view of personal relationships in politics. If you conducted yourself as a friend, he regarded you as a friend. There was no reason why people on opposite sides of the political fence could not be friends (his first appointment to the Supreme Court was a Republican friend from his days in the Senate, Harold Hitz Burton of Ohio). You could be friends and disagree totally on political issues. But you could not be friends with someone who maligned the character of his opponents to gain political preferment. Joseph R. McCarthy of Wisconsin was such a person in Truman's eyes and he would never speak well of him. He believed likewise that Richard M. Nixon had violated the canons of propriety in his campaigns for, first, the House of Representatives and, then, the Senate, and thus he viewed him with deep misgivings.

As a product of the "game of politics" in the United States, Truman viewed politics as a contest rather than a conflict. To be sure, as a lifelong Democrat his mental set favoured the "little man," but there is little in the record of his public (or private) utterances that could be described as of ideological cast. There are numerous indications that he was uncomfortable around people of dogmatic views, be they conservatives, socialists, or liberals. The admiration he held for Franklin Roosevelt was for F.D.R. the pragmatist far more than it was for the proponent of the New Deal. His relationships to any number of fellow senators from both sides of the aisle, both before and after he succeeded to the presidency, fit the same pattern; he appreciated parliamentary workmanship, but, more or less vaguely, suspected ideological rigidity.

This disdain for the dogmatic should not be misunderstood. Truman had (and has) principles and set great story by them. But it is only fair to him to say that his faith was (and is) an affirmation, without many complexities, of the virtues of the society that had nurtured him. In that sense, Truman was always conservative.

But inherent in these virtues was also the spirit of openness that characterized America's western frontier. The visitor who enters the main portal of the Truman Library in Independence, Missouri, faces a floor-to-ceiling mural by Thomas Hart Benton depicting "The Opening of the West"; the theme had been Mr. Truman's personal choice. Historians may (and do) argue about the character of the "frontier spirit" but there is little doubt that it was a reality to those of Truman's generation. In the years of his public schooling, much of what lay west of his home town was still underpopulated or even unpopulated. Oklahoma—the northeast corner of which touches the southwest corner of Missouri—was still legally Indian Territory; Kansas, a mere ten miles west of the hometown of Independence, actively recruited settlers for its "wide open spaces" in England and on the continent. This was country where status counted little and achievement received ready recognition. It was also a setting in which the harshness of conditions imposed a premium on cooperation. Men were judged here on what they could and would do and differences in ancestry, religion or wealth were of secondary importance.

There is much in Truman's record that reflects this attitude that characterized his childhood environment. To be sure, Independence was (and is) a community of southern perspectives. But its geographic location had traditionally given a westward orientation to its thinking and Truman embodied this blend. This was, for instance, evident in his attitude on racial discrimination. It was during his presidency that the first steps were taken, most of them by presidential order, towards the dismantling of the barriers of racial segregation; yet in his retirement years Mr. Truman was occasionally quoted in veins suggesting that he thought the Negro push towards equality had gone too far. What his attitude really was may have been best expressed by a rather brusque reply I heard him give to a student questioner: "Young man, I want every American to have all the rights the Constitution gives him, but I will be the one who decides who eats at my dinner table." As a person, he was saying, I want to judge other persons on a one-to-one basis; society should not compel me otherwise, but neither should it encumber any person with disabilities unrelated to his personal worth.

This emphasis upon personal worth permeates the record of his relationships in public life. There probably were no two people for whom Harry Truman had higher regard than General Marshall and Dean Acheson. Whenever he referred to either of them, in public or in private, it was always in terms of superlatives. Here were two men who commanded his unqualified admiration. They were, as he saw them, men who had given of themselves without stint, men who held no rancour and who measured others by their deeds and not by their words.

Though he admired both and for much the same reasons, there was a marked difference in Truman's relationships to these men. George Catlett Marshall was always "the General." It was not my privilege to see the two men together, but others have related (some with noticeable disapproval in their voices) that Truman always displayed something akin to deference in his conversations with Marshall. Certain it is —because we have Truman's own word for it—that the President had the utmost respect for the General. But Marshall is, of course, one of the few major figures of the forties who commanded virtually universal respect and whose reputation has barely suffered even at the hands of the most critical revisionist historians. Truman's unwavering regard for him is, therefore, hardly conclusive proof for the proposition advanced by some critics that Truman, the First World War captain, was overawed by the Second World War generals. In fact, awe may be one emotion that Truman rarely experienced toward others.

If anyone might occasionally have evoked feelings of awe in Harry Truman, it is more likely that Dean Acheson may have done so. Acheson's exceptional memory certainly impressed Truman deeply and he said so on more than one occasion. In turn, the Secretary of State often remarked on the President's ability to recall things he had read and to assimilate readily what had been put in writing for his perusal. But far beyond this mutual respect, Truman and Acheson had a genuine liking for each other. They were, in many ways, an incongruous pair: Acheson tall, erect, always impeccably groomed, the image of the aristocrat to the manner born—Truman by contrast almost the epitome of the middle class American from the Midwest. Yet no one could be in the presence of these two men without sensing that here was a bond of friendship that far transcended official relationships or even just extended collaboration. Truman and Acheson, it was quite apparent, believed in each other as human beings, as two people who, however different their backgrounds, had arrived at common perceptions of human nature and society.

It may also be that Truman and Acheson agreed so easily because they shared complementary views of their respective roles. Truman's perception of the decisionmaking responsibility of the President has, of course, often been quoted in the capsule version of the sign on his desk, "The buck stops here." Acheson's views have not been given the same pithy coinage but his speeches and writings after he left public office make it quite clear that "responsiblity" was the keyword in his thinking about the presidency.

Yet it is, of course, common knowledge that there were many—perhaps more in the United States than in other countries—who saw Harry Truman in a very different light. Liberal intellectuals in particular had difficulty identifying with the man from Missouri whose speech and manner readily reflected the fact that he was not—as so many of them were—a product of one of the elite colleges on the East Coast. Conservative businessmen were deeply suspicious of the populist heritage evident in the President's views on social and economic issues. In later years it would be said—not entirely in jest—that the difference between Eisenhower, who grew up in a small town in Kansas, and Truman, with his roots in a small town in Missouri, was that Eisenhower had taken up golf while Truman continued to get his exercise by walking.

In the face of these detractions, in the face of almost universal expectations that he would be turned out by the voters, the American people returned Harry Truman to the White House in the 1948 election. The whys and the wherefores of his victory, surprising as it was to apparently everyone but him, have been the subject of numerous books and articles and will undoubtedly continue to be of vexing interest to political historians. In the present context it may be appropriate to note whence the vote for Truman had come. It was avowedly not the vote of wealth nor of the intelligentsia. It was not the vote of the white southerners, so long the mainstay of Democratic politics. It was, rather, the vote of people like Harry Truman himself, people from small farms, people with small businesses, people from small beginnings for whom America as the land of opportunity was an article of faith.

Sidney Hyman, an experienced journalist who can qualify as a "President-watcher" of long standing, devoted a large part of his book *The American President* to the thesis that a successful President is one who appears at a given point in time to personify the inarticulated aspirations of the American people. It would seem—at least—arguable that in November 1948 Harry S. Truman thus found himself embodying what "the little man" projected for his country and for himself. For many others, his success served as an affirmation of a belief in the American political system and its popular base.

Between 1949 and 1952 Truman's popularity was clearly in decline. The reasons were many and complex. He elected—probably wisely— not to seek another term in office and returned to live among his friends in Independence and Kansas City. But not only did he find that a former President never returns to the status of an ordinary citizen; he also soon found that, in retirement, his stature as a President came to receive increasing approval. His willingness to shoulder the responsibility of decisionmaking emerged as a critical contribution to the presidential office; specific decisions of his making were seen as enduring and basic to the nation's course. Whether, in his own words, "it turns out that I was right" is a matter that still awaits the judgement of history. Revisionist historians would urge a negative answer but one could argue that they are writing from a perspective Truman was denied, a knowledge of alternatives enlarged by hindsight.

In his nearly eight years as President of the United States of America Harry S.Truman faced a succession of problems and crises without precedent. His approach was always direct, his objective uncomplicted. He saw himself as a citizen who had been called to serve his country. He viewed his office with unqualified respect while as a person he retained much of the basic traits he had drawn from his early environment. He observed once that he hoped he would be found deserving of a tombstone inscription allegedly seen in a cemetery in a town on the western frontier: "Here lies N.N.—he tried his damnedest." To anyone who knew or knows Harry Truman, there can be little doubt that he offered as an epitaph what he had clearly always viewed as his motto.

A CONCLUDING NOTE

President Harry S. Truman, as much as any American President in modern times, appears to have been the right man for his times. The expansion of the Soviet Union into the empty spaces of Western Europe presented the United States with a grave challenge. Policies were called for to respond at "a turning point in history." Franklin D. Roosevelt's successor proved equal to the task.

As one comes to the end of a series of searching interpretations by political intimates of a President like Harry S. Truman, certain aspects of his strength as a President become clear. To a man his former associates call attention to his political will, courage, self-education and capacity for growth. All that having been said, an air of mystery surrounds a leader such as President Truman. Whence came his strength of character, inner resources and ability to rise to successive challenges? Why was he only a good senator but quite possibly a great President? How was he able to sustain the unflagging respect of colleagues of seemingly far greater intellectual endowments? How could he reach down for insights and resources that had not previously been evident?

After all is said, there is a unique quality to Harry S. Truman, the Missouri politician who became a world leader. The penetrating comments of his close associates help us gain a partial sense of his greatness. But in the end it was Truman, a uniquely individual American, who proved equal to successive challenges and who grew in office. No technique of political analysis can exhaust the mystery of such a personal and political achievement.